ENOUGH!
The College Cost Crisis

How to protect your wallet and your
student's financial future

Bonnie Burkett

ISBN 978-1-7346099-0-5

ENOUGH!
The College Cost Crisis Workbook
(Your FREE bonus gift!)

First of all, a heartfelt thank you for purchasing this book. It is my deep desire that this will assist you and your beloved student on to the right educational path.

Your **BONUS** of the **FREE** student workbook can be downloaded easily at this website.

www.thecollegecostcrisis.com

In this workbook is a chapter by chapter expanded guide for you and your student to work on together.

It will help you:
gather the information you need
work on the various sections
have a place for all your notes.

Please enjoy this gift!

Best Regards,
Bonnie Burkett

Contents

Foreword

We almost couldn't find a college for our kid.

I didn't think it would be so hard. I started getting into the "college thing" when our daughter hit her Junior year in high school. We all knew what she wanted to do. We didn't know where the right programs were, or if they even had them in our state universities.

In her Senior year, we took a well-planned college search road trip and came up empty. A second trip was a bust, too. We had a top-notch student with a clear direction, and she almost couldn't find her school!

Finally, in the last week they were open for the semester, we raced five hours away to her eventual selection. Like everybody else, we stumbled, fell, and crawled to the finish line of getting her launched into college. Eureka! A college and degree program that fit her needs.

Fast forward to her college years. Even with the blessings of two strong scholarships, her net cost to go to a specialty private University was the same as her friends attending in-state universities back home. As I wrote check after check after check, I could not figure out how any family could do this. Or, how any family with more children could afford to do it again and again! I began listening to all the stories—stories of borrowing, stories of default on loans, and scary stories of dropping out with no degree.

There were even more frightening stories over the next few years. Stories of parents stepping in to make the loan payments. Stories of graduated students returning home because they could not find well-paying jobs that covered living expenses AND their student loan payments.

For the past ten years I have been shaking my head, "no". There has got to be another way—another path. Families with financial resources can fund most or all the costs of higher education. For everyone else, it is a mountain they cannot climb. It is not because they don't want to; it is because they don't know critical truths. They don't have the secret knowledge of low-cost options and alternative paths to get that degree without crushing their financial futures.

Getting into college is just the first step. Figuring out how to finish college with the least amount of debt is more important today than EVER before.

With over 1.6 trillion dollars borrowed for higher education, students are going into huge debt at breakneck speed. Elite private schools, such as Duke University, show a sticker price of over $75,000 per year, or right at $300,000 for four years—that is, if you can graduate in four years. Today, a college student has only a 57% chance of getting their degree in *seven years*. Four out of ten students don't graduate, ever. What is going on?

For the past seventy-five years, our American culture has chanted a mantra that **everyone** should go to college. Before World War II, college was reserved for the wealthy and white male segments of our population. With the advent of the GI bill after the war, cadres of service members got their degrees. In the 1960s through 1980s, women and minorities began graduating in larger numbers. Only now, the cost was rising.

Fast forward forty-five years. Since 1975, the cost of living has risen over 300%, while the cost of college has risen over 945%. Let that sink in.

Three out of four students attend public colleges and universities. Most of those schools depend heavily on taxpayer funds to operate. Since the 2008 recession, few public universities have seen an increase in their public funding. In addition, Federal Student Loan money has quietly been trimmed or even eliminated. Yet, money to pay for college must come from somewhere. While students have been borrowing money to go to college for decades, it has reached levels that are crippling to their financial futures.

Before I go any further, let me be clear: I am a HUGE advocate of education beyond the high school diploma.

For most people, a high school diploma is no longer adequate in the 21st century workforce.

I am also a HUGE opponent to the crippling cost visited on unsuspecting students and parents. When college costs ten times what it did fifty years ago, we need to look everything over with a skeptical eye. While some students need a Bachelors' degree AND graduate study for certain career paths and disciplines, others are well suited for the more technical and trades arenas.

Now is the time to DETERMINE which educational path works for *each* of our student(s), our family, and our finances. We MUST take in to account our students' talents and orientations. For some, it could be an education trajectory towards the Bachelors' degree and higher. For others, their interests and gifts may be in the skilled trades. Today, those skilled trades are in very high demand, with no end in sight for the next decade.

The dream of giving your student the same great college or university experience you had may be un-affordable today. Is that experience worth $100,000 in student loan debt? This debt impacts their ability to buy a home or a car, live independently, and move towards their future. This debt is a monthly millstone around their necks for at least ten years. If the loan is refinanced, it can stretch out to twenty-five years. When parents co-sign educational loans for their student, they may be on the hook for repayment if the student fails to do so.

This is the reason I wrote this book for you and those you love. I want you to look at the traditional college path and question it all. Then, be open to alternative paths to the degree or certification that is right for *your* student.

In the first part of the book, I pull back the curtain on the financial costs of attending college **today.** Parents and their students need to look at higher education with a sharp mind and wide-open eyes. You will gain insights into everything that impacts the financial side of college and learn about weighted grade point averages, class rank, and the high bar for most "scholarships". Critical information on how the FASFA works (mostly, against you) is revealed, too.

When you sign on the dotted line to borrow funds, the school gets the money, and you or your student get the bill. That bill must be re-paid, whether your child graduates or not. For nearly four out of ten college students, that is their reality.

In the middle section, I invite you to take a clear-eyed look at your student. How do they approach challenges and tasks? What kind of studies are best suited to your student? Many wonderful, terrific kids are not wired for the classic college route. Some may not be mature enough to handle the array of choices it represents, while others are rarin' to go by their Senior year in high school.

That was true in the past and is still true today. It does not make any sense to co-sign for a $20,000 loan per year, to find all that out. Learning about your teenagers' interests and capacities can help you partner with them towards the right education path. With scary low graduation rates for most schools, getting it right the first time is critical to your wallet.

Finally, I'll show you how to get college credits for pennies on the dollar. This program includes up to two years of college credit courses for less than $3,500. That's right. You can get the basics out of the way for a few thousand dollars! Today, these credits are accepted at over 80% of the colleges and universities in the United States. I'll share many other options for earning a low cost to no-cost college degree, too. Finally, there are three Action Plan Chapters for you to use based on how much money you have available for their education.

Ideally, we all have saved buckets of money for our children's college. Many do, but the amount saved rarely meets the actual need. Since we can't keep up with the current cost trends, let's re-think the entire system.

In today's more complex world, our goal should be to:

- Get them through the RIGHT school;
- at the BEST possible price;
- in the LEAST amount of time;
- that results in a DEGREE or CERTIFICATION they can use.

Knowledge is power. So, power up!

SECTION ONE
The Information You Need
(That They Don't Want You to Know)

Chapter 1

The cost of attending college is killing our children's future. With spiraling, out-of-control, rising costs, it will go from bad to awful in the next few years.

That's because we are in the middle of a perfect higher education storm. This storm is made up of sky-rocketing costs, shrinking government loan programs, and the nearly empty college savings accounts of most families.

In the last fifty years, the cost of attending college has increased by 945%, while the cost of living has increased by just under 300%. The national college loan debt has climbed to over 1.6 TRILLION DOLLARS, with no signs of stopping or slowing down. By comparison, the national auto loan debt stands at 1.1 trillion dollars. Our national credit card debt sits at $1.04 trillion. College loans account for roughly 75% of BOTH our credit card balances AND our auto loans combined. Who knew?

Today's student borrows around $30,000 for their education. It is a debt that must be repaid whether there is a degree at the end of their time in school or not. In fact, every financial aid office says that the single biggest reason for student dropout is overwhelming student debt. This cause has not changed in decades. It was true then, and it is true today.

Unlike decades ago, those loans now take front and center in the life of a graduate OR a dropout. Let's compare: let's say you needed to borrow a total of $5,000 in the late 1970s for tuition and books. Assuming you paid it off over ten years, your monthly payment was about $68 per month. This debt would impact your lifestyle for a few years, but it didn't interfere with your bigger plans as a young adult.

Let's figure out the average monthly payment on a student loan today. Take that national average loan debt of $30,000. The interest rate varies for each type of loan, but let's use the highest, the Parent Plus Loan currently at 7.09%. Over a ten-year period of repayment, the monthly amount is $349.72. And, you will have paid $11,966.15 in interest over that time. This assumes no late payments, ever, and no penalties, either. Just that monthly payment, every month. No. Matter. What.

Folks, that is a car payment. Or, a nice vacation every year. That money could be a fine emergency fund. Or, your buy-a-house-some-day fund. Or, you could have had it matched in your company's 401(k) for a big leg up on your retirement plans. Instead, this monthly bill is an elephant in your life's living room that is there for ten, fifteen or up to twenty five years.

When you sign up for these loans, their impact on your financial future is not discussed in any meaningful way. You are lucky if anyone in the Financial Aid Office says, "Be sure you pay your loans back on time no matter what." Decades ago, these loans were not a part of your personal credit worthiness. Today, they become a part of your personal financial record. Paying your loans in full and on time is mandatory if you hope to keep a great credit score.

As Dorothy says in the movie, *The Wizard of Oz,* we are "...not in Kansas anymore, Toto!". Having student loan debt DOES have an impact on your ability to move forward with life. The financial stress of making timely payments can deeply impact your physical and mental health, too.

Those student loans can make it more difficult to finance a replacement vehicle for your dying car. Even if you have managed your credit to perfection up until then, those loans are a constant for the next 10, 20, or 25 years.

Very few young people I know make a lot of money in their first starter jobs. As they say, if you have more money than month, you done good. In those first entry level jobs, few people find themselves with hundreds of extra dollars at the end of each month.

There is also a silent but harmful impact on students' future retirement nest eggs. Between the ages of eighteen and twenty-seven, every dollar invested in a matching 401(k) will have a spending value of almost $20 when they turn seventy. From age twenty-eight on, they must increase their retirement contributions by 100-200% to make up for any lost years of no contributions. Not taking advantage of matching money in their employer's 401(k) in their earliest years because of high college debt will cost them tens of thousands of retirement dollars fifty years from now.

Freshly minted young people in the workforce face different life decisions because of this debt. As a group, they are waiting longer to have kids (if at all). Many are unable to qualify for a starter home loan unless they have a dual-income household or have stashed away a significant down payment. They don't put any money in to their current employer's 401(k), period. And, the scariest statistic of all, they have less than $1,000 in any type of savings. It is not that they don't want to move forward. They are very clear about their priorities; bills first, future later.

Unfortunately, it can get much worse. Especially if you miss one single payment or stop paying altogether. NOW you are sitting on a financial time bomb. I promise you; it will explode your wallet.

Chapter 2

The government wants its' money back, and it will do anything to YOU to get it.

If you only knew the number of stories I've been told that go something like this...

A student wants a cool sounding job—say, as a video game programmer or graphic designer. After they find a glam school—traditional or for-profit—on the internet, they grab their parent for a visit. Before you know it, the parent agrees to a financial aid package of various loans totaling $15,000 per year after all the discounts and "scholarships" are thrown at you. You and your student sign on the dotted line. They dive in the first year, but discover it is way over their head or interest levels. They crawl and struggle through school that first year. Then they limp back for a second try, taking out another $15,000 loan. At the end of that year, they tell you it is not what they bargained for, and they are quitting school. Fine—or not.

Your now non-student goes out and get an entry level job. It covers the basics, but, that $349/month federal student loan repayment thingy? It's hit or miss, depending on how things look at the end of every month. When you question them, or insist they stay current on it, they shrug their shoulders and say they hope to get a pay raise soon. A few months down the road, a letter arrives, saying the loan is in default.

Whoa. This is where things can go from bad to worse. Much worse.

This important website, https://www.finaid.org/loans/default.phtml, details what happens if you default on student loans. I recommend you read the entire article. Here's THE FOUR most important points YOU need to know about those LOANS.

1. First and foremost, you *cannot discharge* these federal student loans in bankruptcy. For those who have heard otherwise, the percentage of success is 00.4 percent. That is less than 1%.

Take a moment to let that sink in. The debt is forever. It can grow astronomically if you incur penalties for non-payment. Interest is still being tacked onto the loan while it is in a deferral position. A $30,000 initial balance can double or triple if you ignore the demand letters from the government.

2. The "no discharge" rule applies to ANYONE who has signed or CO-SIGNED this loan. That often is a parent, but it could be a grandparent, an uncle, or an aunt.

Let's be very real here. Your signature means that YOU will make the payments if the ex-student does not. Period. No appeals. You are on the hook for this loan, including any penalties and interest. It doesn't matter if the student left school, graduated, doesn't have a job, or doesn't make enough money.

It doesn't matter. You, as a co-signer, are responsible.

3. IF the student defaults on the loan, the government will go after ANY and ALL co-signers.

Failure to pay on time can result in penalties added to your loan balance. If you fail to pay on the loan for nine to twelve months, you are now in default. To prevent even more severe penalties, don't stop payments without first contacting the lender. You need to explain your situation and ask for options. The more you ignore this problem, the worse it becomes! Those penalties get piled on top of the loan and on top of interest. Not addressing the issue can cause the loan to grow much larger and you will be responsible for every penny.

4. What does "go after" mean?

Federal agencies can garnish your *wages,* taking between 15% to 25% from your paycheck. Your employer receives court papers requiring them to withhold the money from your check and sending it to the government coffers for repayment on the loan. They do not have an option. If you are unemployed, they can and will hold back any tax refunds you might have received. Both Federal and private lenders can get court orders to deduct money from co-signers' wages if they cannot get it from the former student.

In order to get any deferral or temporary relief from your payments, you must adhere to the following guidelines:

1. First, talk with your lender(s). Tell them your situation and ask for help and/or options.

2. Get approval for delays in repayment (and get that in writing!).

3. Keep copies of all your communication (emails, letters, etc.) in both print and electronic formats.

4. Document all the payments you have ever made and keep copies of those payments.

Please understand that the school received their money. You and/or your student signed the papers. The debt that you incurred is all yours. Sadly, this gift keeps on giving.

A student loan default hurts your FICO score (the Fair Issacson Company credit score we all have) just like a default on any other loan. Today, FICO has become an integral part of our personal financial lives and future. How you handle your student loans can have some surprising impacts on your life after school!

Here are a few of the "unseen" impacts defaulting on your loan can make.

Professional Licensure

Many occupations such as Attorney, Physician, Accountant, Veterinarian, Insurance Agent, Banker, and Securities Broker have professional governing Boards which "certify" the individual as having met professional standards. Failure to pay on your student loans from any level of higher education may impact your license to practice your profession.

Landing your dream job

Let's talk about the "background review" that impacts hiring decisions. We know that many employers do a "background check". The standard background check includes a review for criminal and civil convictions, but employers often need to know more job-related information. Many positions have access to company credit cards or company vehicles. The employer might include a background check that looks at your financial status or your driving history. A student loan in default could negatively impact you receiving that offer for your dream job.

Getting an affordable car loan

If your clunker car needs replacing, a student loan in arrears or even default can send your FICO score way down. Lower FICO scores do not get the best interest rates on car loans. This means you end up paying much more for that vehicle by being charged higher interest.

Grabbing that first great apartment

Everyone knows that apartment leasing agents run "background checks" on their potential tenants. Included in that check is a review of your criminal history, your credit report, and proof of income as well as eviction and employment histories. Student loans fall under any other credit category. If you have been faithfully making on-time payments of the amount due, that can build your credit score. However, the converse is also true. Multiple late payments, skipped payments, defaults, and other blemishes can drag your score way down. This can hurt your chances at your first apartment.

Buying your first home

The process of getting your first mortgage is even more complex and demanding. If you have any slow or no pays on any loans, they will require a written explanation about what happened and why. The mortgage company wants its' money on-time and it won't stand in line.

The loan repayment requirements begin rather quickly, too. Federal student loans come due six months after you graduate, drop out, or drop below half-time status. Many students receive their notice to start making loan repayments right in the middle of getting a job, relocating for a job, or just staring a job. It can't come at a worse time, because for the most part, it costs money to get started in your new position.

Today, in order to qualify for ANY loans, grants, OR scholarships, every family or student MUST fill out the Free Application for Federal Student Aid, or FAFSA. This application requires very personal financial information that few share with anyone, much less a government entity. It is also the first of many shocks that parents experience in the college-hunting game.

The FAFSA, for many, is one of the greatest eye-opening disappointments you will ever experience.

Chapter 3

FAFSA: It's like playing poker with see-through cards.

In the poker game of college financing today, **you** are the only one at the table with see-through cards.

Artist Cassius Marcellus Coolidge (1844-1934) painted dogs doing every day human activities such as dancing, changing a tire, or enjoying a drink. His most renowned work, "A Friend in Need", shows a poker game attended by various dogs around a table. It depicts two dogs in the foreground of the painting with one passing the other a much-needed illegal ace. In the painting, you can't see any other cards in the game except for the cards of the two dogs down front. In the world of college financial aid, that's not true anymore. Since 1992 when FAFSA started, colleges get a clear picture of your assets, income, and financial capacities. You, dear reader, are the only one at the table with the see-through cards. They know exactly what you've got. And, you don't get to see what they have for you or your student until the financial aid offer letter comes in.

After completing the Free Application for Federal Student Aid process, most parents wish they had an ace or two up their sleeve. This application grabs information from the two years of your tax return prior to the FAFSA application year. In addition, you must divulge personal information such as assets, savings, and investments. At the end, it feels like they know more about you than you know about yourself.

If you need a deep dive into tips and tricks on the FAFSA, please look elsewhere. There is a huge selection of excellent resources on FAFSA strategies on the market already. For example, The Princeton Review publishes an annually updated book, *Paying for College*. I read it. I wish I had read it when our daughter was fourteen years old. If you want to dive into the line-by-line strategies for maximizing your access to loans, this is one of several terrific guidebooks available. In this chapter, we will highlight the most common areas of concern.

The FAFSA 411

No FAFSA—no loans of any kind from the school.

There is a federal methodology for awarding loans or grants. This program reviews the parents' available income and assets, plus the student's available income and assets. Basically, the FAFSA helps the college or university decide what part of your income and assets you can afford to put towards college costs. That is correct. They decide. Every academic year your student needs money to attend college, you will have to fill out a new FAFSA.

When you complete the initial FAFSA, you need to identify every college or university you expect your student will apply to. A list of school codes is provided and the FAFSA results are sent to schools at no cost to you. If another school pops up on your radar, you can add schools later as needed.

Your income look-back period is January Sophomore year thru December Junior year.

The FAFSA looks back at those two calendar years of family income when your student is a Sophomore and Junior in High School. 97% of us don't realize that important fact until the fall or winter of our student's Senior year. Any opportunity to shift or defer income is lost, because you have already filed your taxes. You can't change the numbers you sent in on your tax return, which are the numbers that will be automatically pulled from your tax filings.

The Adjusted Gross Income, line 37, is the number used in the formula.

A key point to remember is that FAFSA does not consider any types of loans you have personally as having any impact on your resources available to pay for college. The formula expects you to use savings, income, and investments to pay your share of the cost of college.

It does not give you a break for needing money to pay on mortgages, cars, or credit card loans.

If your family income is below $25,000 Adjusted Gross Income AND you qualify to file the 1040 EZ, you may qualify for more.

What more do you qualify for? More loans! This gives you access to additional money you can BORROW. You may also qualify for a Federal Pell Grant. The maximum Pell Grant amount is $6,195 for the 2020-21 school year. Again, the methodology calculates the amounts you qualify for in each category. If you get a Pell Grant, that means your family contribution will shrink, But, if you don't have that money, you will have to borrow money to pay the family contribution. This is one of the top reasons why so many students are in such financial dire straits today. Their family finances force them into higher borrowing levels.

Don't put assets into your student's name!

While accountants like to suggest this option to reduce YOUR taxes, it can be very bad at college time. Why? The FAFSA calculates that a student will use 20% of their own assets towards college costs every year. Yikes! Resist putting any significant assets in your students' name because they will be expected to spend it on college tuition.

Don't let your student earn more than $6,600 per year.

The loan formula only considers income above $6,600. The area it hits the hardest are the needs-based grants and scholarships. Unless your student is going to work full time to bank money for college, they should not gross more than $6,600 in a school year. Doing so starts reducing their grants and loans dollars. Keep that part time job, part time.

Expected Family Contribution—a number everyone hates.

One of the most important results from FAFSA is to learn "the number". While the US Department of Education states it is an "index" and NOT the money you actually have to pay, for many families it is very close to what they will need to cover. The Expected Family Contribution is the government's number that you "should" be able to afford towards college. At the very end of the FAFSA application online, you press the button, wait a bit, and the "index" number comes back. It is expressed in 4 to 5 digits with no commas. $11,000 would look like 11000; $7,500 is 7500. In general, this number represents what the government calculates you can bring to the table every year of college. Please note that some pay even more, and some pay less, due to different circumstances.

Best of all? ALL the colleges and universities you have applied to or will apply to, receive a copy of this "index" number. They can all use "the number" to decide how much "other money" you receive. Yessiree, you are the only one at the FAFSA poker game with those see-through cards.

The US Dept of Education just added an online estimating tool called the *FAFSA4caster.* This is a good tool for you use before your student is in the throes of applying for school. It does require you to input all the information about cost to attend a school of choice, plus personal financial details about income and assets. Remember, the further away from actual college enrollment, the less accurate your results will be.

https://studentaid.ed.gov/sa/fafsa/estimate#who-should-use

Another resource for estimating your FAFSA can be found at the website below. Again, this is for your personal practice. It does not count and is not official in any way. It provides a glimpse of what to expect down the road.

https://www.tamingthehighcostofcollege.com/efc

It will only take you 10-15 minutes to get a good idea of what your EFC would be if your child was entering college *today.* **The further away your student is from starting college, the less likely it will be accurate.** That said, give it a try. It will help you understand why you must help your student do college as close to debt-free as possible.

Turn to the next page for a graphic chart of three fictional families and their practice FAFSA numbers. I ran each "family" through the practice FAFSA calculator which then gave their expected family contributions for the first year of college. I chose three University campuses in my state of North Carolina, USA—the flagship campuses—UNC-Chapel Hill and NC State, and a regional University campus, UNC-Charlotte. I used the most current in-state tuition rates, too. To keep it simple, all the other numbers were filled in realistically.

Three Samples of FASFA Results @www.tamingthehighcostofcollege.com/efc			
Core FASFA Questions	Jones Family	Davis Family	Smith Family
Family Information			
Number Of Parents	2	2	1
Age of Parents	40	48	1
# of In-College kids	1	1	1
Total People in HH	4	5	2
Family Income			
Ajsdt Gross Inc (AGI)	$100,000	$70,000	$48,000
Ret Cntrb this year	$6,000	$3,000	$1,000
Child Support	$0	$0	$4,200
Tax-free Income	$0	$0	$0
Parent 1's Income	$125,000	$45,000	$60,000
Parent 2's Income	$0	$40,000	$0
Fed Income Tax Pd	$22,000	$13,000	$10,000
Parent Assets			
Bank Accounts	$3,000	$2,000	$1,000
Investments	$75,000	$30,000	$5,000
Real Estate Net Value	$45,000	$20,000	$10,000
Trusts	$0	$0	$0
College 529/Ed IRA's	$6,000	$0	$0
Business/Farm	$0	$0	$0
Other	$0	$0	$0
Student Assets	$0	$0	$0
Student Assets			
Student Income	$0	$0	$0
Student Assets	$0	$0	$0
Cost of Attendance/Yr	$26,000 (UNC-CH)	$24,500 (NC State)	$22,500 (UNC-Char)
Estimated EFC	$19,582	$4,169	$3,344
Estimated Fin Need	$6,418	$20,331	$19,156

At the bottom are two lines; your Estimated Financial Contribution (EFC), AND your estimated financial need. The financial need line will be offered loans through the federal programs available.

Here's what you MUST remember about the Estimated Financial Contribution. **If you don't have that**

money, you will have to borrow that, too! You can end up financing BOTH your EFC and the unmet financial need. It's not one or the other; it can be BOTH numbers in your first-year loan. If you are extremely lucky, it only happens three more times and they GRADUATE with a useful degree. But what if it doesn't work out that way?

Let's summarize: you submit your FAFSA that gives you an "index" number that often becomes the amount you need to pay. Then there is federal loan money for BOTH the unmet financial need, AND the Expected Family Contribution index number. And finally, you will have to re-submit the FAFSA every year until the student is no longer in school to receive any loans.

But, wait. What about scholarships? So glad you asked. Scholarships misinformation will hurt anyone and everyone.

Chapter 4

Scholarships—the dirty little secrets no one tells you.

Good students get into colleges; very few will get the coveted Willy Wonka Golden Ticket.

In the classic movie, Willy Wonka and the Chocolate Factory (1971), little Charlie finds one of five golden tickets in his chocolate factory for a chance to become the heir to the Wonka chocolate bar. As everyone knows, Charlie is finally chosen after going through a series of "tests" to determine his worthiness.

You can say that the world of scholarships is just about as strange as the Wonka Chocolate Factory. The range of stories runs the gamut from "millions are left un-applied for" to, "my straight A student didn't get a single scholarship offer". How can these both be true?

Let's agree on the definition of what scholarship means. It is a grant or payment made to support a student's education, awarded on the basis of academic or other achievement.

Time to look at the national data.

Every year approximately 3.1 million high school students graduate from 37,100 high schools in the United States. In 2016, 69.7% of those graduates enrolled in some type of post-secondary education! (TED: The Economics Daily, May 22, 2017) That is over two-thirds of every high school graduating class going to some type of college.

By comparison in 1975, barely over 50 % of all high school graduates enrolled in some form of college (https://nces.ed.gov/programs/digest/d99/d99t187. asp). Since 1975, there has been a 40% increase in those entering college. While we celebrate this number, it means something more difficult for each of us. The *competition* for any grants or scholarship money has increased by that same 40% in the last forty years.

This means there are MORE people competing for all kinds of scholarships. If you used to be in a scholarship pool of, say, fifty people, your group has grown to seventy. Combine that with reduction in taxpayer dollars being pumped into public universities, and you have a squeeze in available funds.

Let's cover the most well-known areas for scholarships: Academic, Sports, and the Arts.

Academic Scholarships

Most people tie academic performance to the concept of scholarship. Before we go any further, let's do some basic math. As noted, there are 37,100 high schools in the United States. At every graduation ceremony, the salutatorian (second-highest grade point average) and the valedictorian (highest grade point average) students are introduced. In other words, 74,200 students graduate high school each year in first and second place in their class.

Oh, and by the way, there are roughly 5,300 colleges and universities in the United States.

If the top two students from every high school were *evenly* distributed across all the college campuses in the country, there would be seven valedictorians and seven salutatorians on every campus. Now, we know that's not the case. However, it is possible they might have a #1 or #2 position student in any freshman class. Academic scholarships are offered to those students with a demonstrated skill at academics. If your student wants to compete for academic money, they will need to very well over their three or four years in high school.

There are three arenas which play a big role in obtaining an academic scholarship:

- strong ACT/SAT scores,

- terrific grade point averages, plus the latest emphasis,

- your class rank.

ACT/SAT Scores

Let's start with the ACT scoring method. Your student takes the test and receives a number between 1 and 36, which reflects the percentile they attained. By math definitions, a percentile is a comparison ranking between your student and ALL the other students who took the ACT that year. It does not mean you got X number of questions right or wrong. It is a comparison ranking among all the ACT test takers across the country who took that specific test.

Please remember that every college or university has their own ideal target range of student scores. Each school reviews students for their institutional needs and profile. For example, a flagship university may only target the top fifteen percentile for admissions. A private college down the road may offer scholarships to the top thirty-five percentile. Why the variance? The private school wants to attract people, but they are competing against the bigger University nearby. So, you ask, what kind of score might earn an academic scholarship?

For perspective, a score of 20 on the ACT is usually considered to be in the middle. Scores at 27 and above can start seeing partial academic scholarship offers. This is subject to each student's grade point average and their class rank being at the same relative level as their ACT score. Remember, it is not one thing; it is all about your total package.

Now let's move into the SAT. Since 2016, the SAT has returned to the traditional total maximum points of 1600. The writing section has now been made optional. The final score is a composite of two area scores; Evidence based reading & writing, and math which focuses on the core algebra concepts.

In today's hyper competitive market, it is important to do as well as possible on either the SAT or ACT. In general, an SAT score of 1200 and above may get you some academic scholarships. A score at 1400 or above should put you in the running for the larger academic awards.

Before your student takes this long and hard test for the first time, consider having them take the PSAT in their Sophomore year. The PSAT test results report your student gets online will give you information about their strengths and weaknesses in testing. The College Board's partnership with Khan Academy provides free training for the SAT. Khan Academy is highly regarded in the online education space. In addition, there are professional ACT/SAT prep programs online and at local learning centers, but they charge fees. Being able to take a tough national test and do well is essential for earning academic scholarship funds.

Class Rank and Grade Point Averages

There is a trend in college admissions criteria that is gaining favor across the country. Over 1,000 colleges and universities no longer require either the ACT or SAT tests for admission purposes. Currently, colleges are moving towards class RANK as a better predictor of your eventual college graduation. Why is this important? As a parent or guardian, you need to know HOW your student's class rank is calculated, because it may have changed since you were in school!

When I was in high school, it was simple; an A got four points, a B got 3 points, and so on. We usually knew what our grade point average was and how it was calculated. This was because all the courses had the same points values.

Times and high schools have changed. When Honors courses, Advanced Placement, or International Baccalaureate studies were added to the curriculum, many high schools changed to a weighted grade point average.

You need to do your homework in your back yard on this issue. Find out exactly what kind of grading system your student's high school uses, so you are not fooled. I have had proud parents sit in my office bragging about their kid having a 3.9 grade point average in my local school system. I knew that our schools used a three-tier rating system that results in a weighted grade. While that is a nice grade point average, it is not even close to a top student's grade point average in a weighted grading system. A nearly straight-A student may score a 4.83 or higher in a three-level weighted system. It is critical you know how to interpret your student's grades in **your** local grading system.

Not all Grade Point Averages are Equal

Traditional Scoring: A= 4.0; B= 3.0; C= 2.0. If you earn a 3.5 GPA, it meant you were averaging mostly A's and B's. This system has been in place the longest.

Weighted Grade Point System: Confirm the kind of class your student is taking AND the scale used to grade it. The actual point "spread" varies across the country.

Sample Weighted High School Course Values

Regular High School Classes: An A equals a 4.0

Honors High School Classes: An A means a 4.5

Advanced Placement or IB Classes: An A means a 5.0

To calculate your student's grade point average, you need three pieces of information:

1. Your student's course level: Regular, Honors, or Advanced?

2. Grade earned and grade point value in that specific class;

3. Total amount of high school classes taken to date.

First, keep a copy of every report card. On each report card, have your student identify the "level" of each course, and put the corresponding grade value beside it. Then, add all the grade values together, and divide that by the number of classes they have taken to date. This should result in a grade point average. This calculation must be re-done every time a new grade report comes out.

Class rank is determined by the difficulty of the course, multiplied by the grade of the course, with all the courses added up, then divided by the number of classes taken. Then, they are ranked in descending order against the grades of all the other students in her or his class.

At my daughter's high school district, we were very fortunate that we did not have to do the above calculation. Twice a year—in teeny-tiny print, in the corner of the report card—we would see a box with a number that read, "136 of 381". The first number is your student's class position or rank. The second number is the total number of students in the class. Both numbers change over time because the number of students in her class changed, and, the grades she earned impacted her ranking. Your student's ranking can go up or down every semester. From the first day of high school to the final grade of senior year, it matters how your student approaches their academic work.

The Bottom Line: Get to the truth about your student's classes, grades, class standing and REAL grade point average. You can impact their grade point average much easier at the end of their first semester as a freshman than in the fall of their senior year. To earn an academic scholarship, your student should be aiming as high as possible. The competition is fierce these days.

Sports Scholarships

I believe in the positive effect sports can have on our kids. If you have the means and your student loves their sport, support their interests. Sports teaches teamwork, time management, and strong interpersonal skills. I know the value sports bring and have enjoyed them throughout my life.

But there is another aspect to all of this. Talented student athletes are courted for higher and higher levels of amateur sports teams. Often, a well-intended coach sees professional potential and mentions the magic phrase: "college athletic scholarship". This can lead some families to build their lives around higher levels of travel ball. They are seeking that illusive Division I or a Division II athletic scholarship.

While *your* student may be one of the fortunate few to receive such an offer, you need to know how special that really is. I want you to think long and hard on this sobering truth:

Only 2% of all high school athletes ever get an athletic scholarship offer. Of those that DO get an offer, the average amount is *$11,000 per year or less*. (CBS News, May 22, 2012 article)

Even IF your student is the exception, it rarely covers more than one-third to one-half of college tuition, and room and board these days.

A manager I work with has a talented volleyball student-athlete. She played on her high school team as well as five years of increasingly difficult travel ball. When it was time for those athletic scholarship offers, they were very consistent. Regardless of the actual cost of attending a school, the scholarship offer was less than one-third of the overall cost to attend. As we were talking, I filled in the one-third number and the maximum of $11,000. He looked bewildered and asked, "How did you know?".

I knew because those are the rules as established by the NCAA for Division I and II schools. No athletic scholarships are awarded by Division III schools to incoming athletes. Other scholarships such as academic or leadership are available at Division III schools.

If your student attends a high school that fields a football, basketball, and baseball team, and plays on one of those teams, consider these numbers:

- High School football teams vary widely across the country in their roster count. But it is safe to say rarely more than one person per team will earn a Division I or II athletic scholarship.

- High School baseball rosters are up to twenty players, so only 1 student out of 2.5 teams would likely receive some level of college sports scholarship.

- High School basketball teams have fifteen players on their rosters, which means that barely one player in four teams might earn an athletic scholarship.

It is even harder to receive a scholarship in other sports, known in college speak as "equivalency" sports. These are the sports which are revenue eaters, not revenue generators. Some examples may include tennis, rowing, lacrosse, volleyball, field hockey, and swimming. This is not meant to disparage these great sports. However, they simply don't generate the revenues that the larger programs do.

As hard as it is to earn a college athletic scholarship, the mountain is nearly impossible beyond college.

Only 2% of college athletes ever go professional.

So, only 2% of the 2% will ever get a professional paycheck. Even the NCAA has provided a television commercial confirming this statement. I believe most of us would agree we can "spot" most of these superstar high school athletes easily. Their talent and drive shines above just about everyone else.

A few years back, a local athlete burst on the high school football scene. He helped lead a brand-new high school to the 4-A state championships. He had blinding speed. The only question was where he was going to go. To everyone's surprise, he followed a friend out to the University of California, Berkeley, where he broke records for three years. In 2013, he was drafted by the San Diego Chargers. Everyone knew this guy could go pro, and he did. His name? Kenan Allen.

There is nothing wrong with being proud of our children's talents and hard work. It is one of the best rewards of being a parent. We need to be the wise ones, though; armed with the facts. It is critical you have a clear understanding of your student's athletic scholarship chances in the world of college sports.

Arts Scholarships

All activities to do with music, dance, and visual arts come under this classification. Unfortunately, there is very little money available for arts scholarships—much less full financial rides. In most programs, there may only be enough money to attract one or two top talents.

The daughter of a family friend had a good voice. She sang solos and was selected for a prestigious chorus. Deciding she wanted to major in voice, she applied and was accepted into a top-notch state University program. My friend knew that all voice majors were required to pass a piano proficiency test and shared this with her. The student had never taken piano, but with the help of a good piano teacher, could have tackled this requirement over the summer. She did not do so. After one semester, she left the program and the school, citing overwhelming demands of the program. She had not prepared ahead of time for the rigors of this well-regarded program, or used her free time wisely.

If your student shows special gifts in an arts area and wants to pursue it professionally, confirm these three aspects:

First, have they taken or studied their art at the middle and high school level?

Most arts students need to learn and grow in their gifts. They often become lost in their work and the practice of their arts studies.

I had a Junior in high school in my office for a visit, and before we started, I asked him if he had any colleges in mind. He said yes, he was looking at a "cool school" out of state that offered a major in videogame development.

Unbeknownst to him, I had learned a little about that major, and asked him, "Which side do you want to do, the coding or the art?"

He was surprised at the question, and stammered back, "Uh, the art side, 'cause I like to draw some."

I responded with, "Great! How many art classes have you taken so far in high school?"

His reply? "Uh, none."

I said, "I am sure they will want you to have an art portfolio to show them."

His parent, surprised, said to him, "You have an elective or two; you can take the art classes you need."

Then I asked him about his grades and related stuff. His parent immediately responded by saying he had no study skills and hated high school. It was not a promising answer. End result? He did not attend the cool school.

Arts are a wonderful enrichment in our lives. Whatever level you can do, I encourage you to be involved.

But, when you want to make your art your career, you must take the necessary steps to determine if you have the right stuff. That stuff consists of talent AND discipline, hard work AND teachability, and an unquenchable desire to keep getting better at your craft.

Learning your art is a part of your passion: learning requires discipline and focus.

Second, are they winning awards and growing in skills?

Native or natural talent is a part of what makes an artist. Only when that talent is joined with the work ethic and the drive to get better does it blossom into success. When these three elements come together, talent, work ethic and drive, it shines brightly for others to see. Students who receive awards by judges and are recognized by their peers, generally have all three critical elements.

Third, does your student demonstrate an overwhelming desire to work at their art expression?

When you are called to an art form, you want to do it all the time. You want to improve; you want to watch, see, and be with similar artists to learn more. Here are some tips for parents of serious arts students.

Get in touch and stay in touch with their teachers and instructors in their arts field. Listen carefully to how your student's teachers describe their art, work ethic and talent.

I was very blunt with my daughter's art teacher. I said I did not want kindness; I needed truth. I asked her point blank if our student had what it would take to do college in her chosen field. She looked me in the eye and said yes. THEN, I asked her **why** she believed that. She was able to give me great examples. This soothed my need to understand so I could help my student find the right school.

If you see your student with all these traits, consider these ideas to deepen their arts experience.

- Try to find ways to afford your student exposure to various aspects of their art form. Local summer arts courses may be affordable.

- Some arts programs offer "scholarships" based on financial need. Don't be afraid to ask! Many thresholds are more generous than you may realize.

- Look for reduced cost "student" focused programs in your students' arts area, and take them to performances, art shows and other related events.

- Connect your student to volunteer opportunities in their arts area. This will help them see the "work side" of their area of interest.

Regardless of their interests, there is a day for you and your student when the "rubber meets the road." That is the day you receive the college financial aid letters. If you have never had a student get one of these things, it looks like a jumble of numbers, letters, and words. Each letter from each school will do their offers in a different order. Each letter looks different. How will you know who is making the best offer? How can you ask for more money? How can you leverage a better offer from the school of your choice?

The time to train on this is BEFORE you start receiving those offers. Let's make you a confident expert on college offer letters!

Chapter 5

*The College Offer Letter: it contains more puzzle categories than the game show **Jeopardy**!*

Let's set the stage. Your student worked hard in high school, applied to a few universities and colleges, but has their heart set on The One School. You've waited for delivery of The Letter, which often comes today by Electronic Notification. Whether they click a button or slit open an envelope and it says, "Congratulations!", it is a Red-Letter Day! The notification goes on to say something like, "We are pleased to welcome you to the Class of 20XX", blah, blah, blah. At the end, they tell you to be on the lookout for your separate letter/email explaining all your grants, scholarships and Financial Aid options.

A few days later, here comes the fat envelope or another electronic letter. You rip it open, expecting to see a windfall of grants and scholarships. Instead, it is a bunch of confusing numbers with words like Expected Family Contribution, Federal Unsubsidized Loan, Federal Subsidized Loan, Parent Plus Loan, and other strange terms. What exactly does it all mean? It means it's time to become well trained at deciphering these numbers.

Spoiler Alert

All financial aid letters should be required to follow a standard format so a student and their family can compare offers. Unfortunately, there is NO requirement for the way financial awards letters are written. Colleges and universities are free to create their own, and some do. However, lots of schools use a patterned letter that covers the subject in roughly this order. Let's take a walk through these sections.

A. **Table of Costs**—or the "projected" cost of attendance—includes, tuition, fees, and room and board. It is broken down by "on-campus" residency, and "off-campus" residency. Housing and meals for off-campus living costs are based on averages nearby and are just the colleges' best guess.

B. **The Expected Family Contribution** is clearly labelled. According to the US Dept of Education, this is an "index" number and not exactly what you would pay. However, it is the amount they will exclude from needs-based lending options. If you are receiving the awards letter from a private school, there could be a second number that came from another calculation process used by private schools.

C. Any area labelled **Scholarships** and **Grants** is golden. This is money awarded to your student that does not have to be repaid. Remember, most scholarships have some form of performance attached to them. This can be maintaining a certain grade point average, or remaining eligible to play on a team, or other privileges. Make sure you and your student are clear on what the rules are. If your student does not hold up their end of the deal, the scholarship can and will be withdrawn.

D. Any line or category that uses the word **Loan** is the most important to understand. This is money you are borrowing, so it must be paid back. Remember, you can accept or reject any parts of student financial aid offer, including those loans.

E. **Loan Options**. Four such options are described below.

1. **Federal Direct Subsidized Loan** @ x.xx interest rate

    Your student's eligibility for this loan is based on NEED, as determined by your FAFSA and the government formula. IF you *qualify,* you can borrow money from the government, and while your student is in school, the government pays the interest on the loan. If this area is blank, you do not qualify for this type of student loan.

2. **Federal Direct Unsubsidized Loan** @ x.xx interest rate

    This money is available to your student regardless of financial need. Anyone can apply for this loan. However, interest is accrued (added to the loan) every year. That means if you take a loan out for their freshman year, interest is added on for their sophomore, junior and senior years, too. It can impact the total amount owed very quickly over four years. The university you attend determines the maximum amount you can borrow.

3. The next big loan option is the **Parent Plus Loan,** offered directly to the parents of the student. Your repayment can be on a fixed ten-year plan, a graduated payment plan (less now, more later), or an extended repayment plan of up to twenty-five years.

4. **Private Loans** @x.xx interest rate.

   The private market for parents to borrow for their student's college is complex and very fluid. The top reasons to consider a private education loan is because you need more money than you are being offered, AND you have excellent credit. Qualifying for private education loans requires a strong level of credit worthiness, too. Review all your other options before going into this arena.

F. **Grants,** unlike scholarships, are not generally based on academics. Grants are generally based on financial need as determined by the formula(s) calculated by the government. For some students, there will not be anything in this section.

G. **Net Costs.** This is calculated by subtracting the scholarships and grants sections from the Total Cost of Attendance. This is the money you must either pay out of pocket or borrow.

H. **Work-Study Options.** These are awarded by the school on a federally calculated needs basis. They are given at the discretion of each school within their respective guidelines. Please don't be surprised if there is nothing here. Each school makes the final decision in this area.

The College Awards letter is not easy to understand. Period. The best way to compare offers is to put them in to a spreadsheet. Your spreadsheet can be on a computer or a notepad. Just be sure you use one. It is a big decision. Take your time to do it right. Don't be hasty.

Don't forget these important issues:

Deadlines are Critical!

College financial aid letter offers all have deadlines by which you must respond. This is critical! If you get an offer from school A, but your student has their heart set on school B, here's what you do: Call school B and ask them to get their offer out to you immediately. Accept an email offer to save mail time.

Negotiate!

If your top school choice is less generous with money, but your student can't see themselves anywhere else, call the Financial Aid Office. Tell them how much your student wants to attend. If you have a better offer from school B, let school A know that. They may ask to see your "offer letter" from the competing school, but it may also result in a "revised" offer from school A. Don't forget to ask for the revised offer as soon as possible.

Review Resources!

Evaluate your own financial resources to determine where you will take money for college payments. Some households tap into their home equity, others their savings, and some, investments. If this looks impossible, hold on. Options will be shared soon!

Why cover this now? Many of you don't even know where your student might go. To reduce the shock in the future, you need to know today what it will cover. This also provides time for you to become familiar with the sections. With your new knowledge, those offer letters will be much easier to understand.

Before the offers arrive, be crystal clear on *why your student* should go to college. Ask these questions:

- Is going to XYZ college more important to me or my student?

- Is my student clear on their educational path, goals, and the work required to meet those goals?

- Have I shared the rules for my student to remain in college and the "Plan B" if they cannot meet the family requirements to remain in school?

Few families can afford to send their students off to college with no strings attached. My parents sat me down and said they expected a certain grade point average over my college career. If I could not commit to do the work at that level, I could come home to a "Plan B". When Plan B was explained to me, it was terrible! I made sure there would **never** be a need to go in that direction. Ever.

College or university is too expensive today to be taken lightly. We are surrounded by "myths" or beliefs that can deeply influence our decisions about higher education and our students. Some of our beliefs come from things our parents said to us. Others come from society and cultural pressures. Education expectations as well as cultural myths can deeply impact our financial decisions. Before you agree to borrow money, take a careful look at your long-held beliefs in light of the costs, graduation data, and your family's resources.

What are some of the myths or education expectations in your family or among your friends?

Chapter 6

If your time to you Is worth savin'
Then you better start swimmin'
Or you'll sink like a stone
For the times they are a-changin'

—**Bob Dylan,** songwriter

We all come to the college education landscape with two sets of ideas swirling around in our minds and our hearts. They are education expectations and myths.

Education expectations are the beliefs we hold for ourselves or our students. Those are the quiet dreams, longings, and ideas you may cherish deep, deep in your heart. For example, you may want your student to be the first in your family to go to college. Or, your student may be expected to be the fourth generation to attend dear old ALMA U. Some parents believe going to college makes their student bullet proof in life. Or, sometimes it can stem from the simple belief that "my student is just as good as the neighbors' kid, so I will do whatever it takes to get them into *that* college with everyone else". Many of us don't even know what our education expectations are.

Myths can often be carried by people from generation to generation. If stated often enough, by enough people, they become a cultural Truth. Frequently, they were true in their time. While times have changed, our societal myths have not stayed current with the changes around us. Let's explore a few of the most common myths swirling around higher education.

Myth #1: Any college degree is better than none.

There is still some of truth in this statement. AS A GROUP, college graduates earn more money than some other groups of students. However, there are many more paths to financial success today than just through the traditional college and university processes.

First, there is the assumption that all college degrees bring the graduate more income than their non-college peers. Today we know that is not true in many service professions, especially teaching, public service work, and similar vocations.

Second, many technical positions pay quite well today, and are highly sought after by many companies. It is well worth your time to review those options in your locale if your student has a gift in that area.

Third, no student will do well in something that does not engage their interests. The myth that "any degree is better than no degree" needs to be buried. Let's focus on getting the RIGHT educational training for the student.

Myth #2: **I want my kid to have the same wonderful college experience I had.**

For many of us, college was a mosaic of great fun times and hard marathon studies. We worked, laughed, worried, and learned life lessons together. In large and small schools, there were opportunities to meet and form lifelong relationships on our campuses. And, there is the known truth that the further away we are from that time, the rosier the memories.

Times and wallets look a lot different today.

To be blunt, it is very unlikely your student will have anything close to the experience you had twenty, thirty or even forty years ago. College today is significantly more expensive and demanding, and students must manage themselves with strong discipline. Remember this; you are giving them your beloved student AND your hard-earned money. Look carefully at all the options, including costs and graduation rates. Interview THEM to see if they are the right fit for your student in all respects.

Myth #3: **In OUR family we always attend XXX College or University.**

I know for many, there is only ONE place their student is going to school, period. Many venerated institutions deeply appreciate it, too. In fact, they are often counting on the year your student is eligible to enter college. Your student is called a legacy. Sometimes, they may provide a modest "legacy" discount for your student, but it rarely dents the current costs of attending your alma mater. And sometimes, our alma mater, large or small, is NOT a good fit for our student.

I went to a small private college back in the day. They started recruiting our daughter in her sophomore year. Because she was a good student, they'd send someone by my office to chat about her every six months. By her Senior year in high school, it was clear she needed a very specific major for her career. They didn't have it. On the fourth in-person visit, I had to kindly and firmly explain that we could not consider my alma mater for her—period. The offer to "work out some kind of major like what she might need", didn't cut it. The university she graduated from was designed for the work she is doing to this day. It was the right decision for her future.

Myth #4: Alternate educational paths are for losers, with the capital "L".

Wow. It makes me sad there are still some folks thinking that way. Great students are getting terrific, well-paying jobs through community college skilled training programs. Almost every community college around the country is partnered with local industry, manufacturing, and high-tech businesses to train the workforce of the future.

According to Adecco, a nationwide hiring company, upwards of five million skilled trades positions will be vacant by 2020. The starting pay in many entry positions rivals or exceeds a starting teacher's salary. You can find terrific training programs that pay your tuition and pay you while you learn. Then, they find companies who stand in line to offer you a job when you finish with your certification.

Additionally, some believe that attending the first two years at community college, and then using the transfer program into "big" college, means you are not as smart as others. Let's get another perspective. The student who works and attends community college, paying their way as they go, might be the one with the smarts. Or, the student who does two years online from a computer, works part-time, and saves enough to pay for the final two years of college? That student may be a financial genius.

Today, smart students and their parents look at all their options for getting to and through college. Personal management skills are essential for handling your studies, your life, and your future. In the next section, we'll explore those necessary skills as well as the unique ways your student works in the world.

Getting into college is one thing. Thriving in college takes a specific skill set. The good news? Those skills can be learned, practiced, and make a BIG difference in your results!

Identifying and Educating into Your Student's Gifts

Chapter 7

Does your student know and practice ALL the skills needed for college success?

I have never met a parent who is not passionate about their student. You love them—deeply. You want the best for them; no question about that. You want to help them be their best, do their best, and launch well into the world. But you don't know HOW to help them with all that.

For the most part, neither do they. But I am sure of one thing. The foundation of success in college is the ability to manage academic challenges. Without academic skills, college will overwhelm them, and they will do poorly or drop out, or both. That is why it is so important to start with the issue of academic skills.

To get a leg up on your student's college capacities, consider this simple process. It can apply to the range of skills needed for school. First, ASSESS (evaluate) your student's skills in a given arena. Second, ADDRESS (identify) any areas that need your help. Third, COACH (provide guidance) for any missing essential skills needed. If coaching your student's needs is beyond your capacity, reach out to her/his teachers, counselors, or your schools' academic tutoring program.

Academic Proficiency is THE skill required for college success today. There are two distinct segments:

A. Reading and Comprehension, and

B. Math Fluency.

Let's start with the core skills of Reading and Comprehension. Most students who graduate from high school can read, but not everyone has mastered the comprehension side of learning.

In the article, "Teach the Seven Strategies of Highly Effective Readers", author Elaine L. McEwan shares there are seven active processes going on in strong readers:

"A. ACTIVATING—Pulling stuff from long-term memory that will help you understand.

B. INFERRING—Pulling together old knowledge, what is written + what is known.

C. MONITORING-CLARIFYING—Thinking about what you read and after you read, to be sure you understand what is being shared, and find stuff that doesn't add up.

D. QUESTIONING—Engaging in conversations with peers, teachers or in your head with the author.

E. SEARCHING-SELECTING—Checking cited sources or other resources to clarify any concerns or questions.

F. SUMMARIZING—Restating the meaning in one's own words (that you got from your own mind, not someone else's thoughts you heard)

G. VISUALIZING-ORGANIZING—Developing a mental image or graphic design that constructs meaning for the student to be able to easily remember it."

More information about teaching Reading Comprehension can be found on his website: www.adlit.org/article/3479.

These seven active processes demonstrate the techniques needed to master the reading load in most colleges today. In addition to Reading Comprehension, the ability to research topics and properly cite your sources, is critical to academic success.

Why is this at the top of the list? Even the best students may not know HOW to read for knowledge. A key difference between most high school courses and college classes is the latter focus on critical thinking and analytical processes. In high school, you tend to recite facts. In college, many courses examine the reason behind an event or idea. Reading Comprehension is important as we all move through careers and need to learn and re-learn to stay current.

Along with Reading and Comprehension comes the importance of Math Fluency. Even though one of our cultural myths is that either you have a "head for numbers" or not, that is not correct. It is a skill that is teachable and acquirable.

Math Fluency is critical, whether you are going to college or not. According to a 2006 study by the ACT, anyone learning a technical skill needs a sound foundation in core math skills to make themselves employable.

In a May 2018 article found at https://www. greatschools.org, Professor W. Stephen Wilson at Johns Hopkins University and a former senior advisor for mathematics in the U.S. Department of Education's Office of Elementary and Secondary Education, talks about the essential mathematical skills needed after high school to survive either college or the workforce.

"Arithmetic. You really have to be able to add, subtract, multiply, and divide with pencil and paper, do ratios, propositions, and percentages, and work multi-step word problems that apply arithmetic." Then he ticks off the list of classes a college-bound student should take; "... algebra I, geometry, algebra II and some trig".

The natural affinity between science and math is obvious, but math by itself is critical also. Anything related to coding, computers, programming, software design, video game design, data analytics, and many other fields require a solid foundation in math.

In addition to these formal mathematical disciplines, you must teach your student fundamental "life math".

This includes how to read their bank statement; create a student budget; understand credit card debt, and other basic financial management principles. Without this knowledge, they can easily fall victim to financial scams aimed at college students like themselves. Working out financial budgets for their time in college is important for both the parent and the student.

Another critical issue in managing college is Time Management.

You may be thinking, "Wait a moment. My student is doing fine right now. She or he is making good grades in high school and has plenty of time for video games, activities, and friends." Indeed. Most high school students have learned some time managing skills. Nevertheless, they generally have a village around them helping with things like laundry, food, reminders for project due dates, help getting out of bed, and everything else. You know what I am saying, because you know all you do to help your student. One of the critical issues for all students, especially those in their first year, is learning the art of Time Management.

Let me share with you an article from the https://www.thecollegeinvestor.com, in October 2017, by Robert Farrington: He says:

"A great example of how to master time management is given in Cal Newport's book, *How to Become A Straight A Student.* Here is a summary of what he suggests when it comes to time management.

'There are only 2 things you need when it comes to managing your time: a list of all your activities (curricular and extra-curricular) for the semester and a calendar/planner.

Once you determine what deadlines fall on what dates for assignments that are due in your classes, you can then begin to place each of these items on your calendar.

Once you have a 'big picture' look of where everything falls on your calendar, it is now time to organize those activities by a daily schedule with assigned times.

Now that you know what your daily schedule looks like for each day of the week, it is up to you to follow the activities you have set forth to the 't' so you are not scrambling to complete assignments the night before it is due.

A handy time management skill for completing tasks—especially if it is not a class but a self-driven activity like completing homework assignments—is to set a timer for 45 minutes to 1 hour and focus on working on the assignment only during that time. During this 45-60-minute time frame, you will turn off social media, your cell phone or cut out as many distractions around you as possible. This period is for deep work. When your timer goes off, you are free to get up, stretch, take a walk or take a break before you return. Do this for a 2-3-hour time block each day and you will be amazed at how far ahead you are come semester's end!"

Easy, right? Yes, it is. It is ESSENTIAL to surviving and thriving in your first year at school. Does your student practice this time and life management program today? Putting classes, work, study and free time on their calendar can improve any student's daily task management. Of course, things happen that impact a schedule. When you work your own plan, you will be able to take advantage of great last-minute opportunities, because you have made good progress on your work all along.

While these specific skills are critical to their academic performance, there is something else even more valuable. There is something so powerful within in us that it can make or break us in our careers, social skills, and life management. Scientists are now saying this factor is MORE important than one's Intelligence Quotient (IQ).

What could that be? Emotional Intelligence (or Quotient). Some call this EQ.

We've all encountered someone who is naturally good with people. We have known someone with limited educational opportunity who is exceptionally successful. They are successful with friends, family, and career. Sometimes, they seem too good to be true. Chances are, they are very talented in the Emotional Quotient core skills areas.

Your student can benefit immensely by learning about emotional life skills that are critical to their future success. In fact, why not do this process together? Investing in this area with and for your student will result in several bonuses in your relationship to each other:

1. It can open up conversations outside of the parent/student role.

2. It is any easy way to compare notes—and often laugh with each other!

3. It may encourage them ask for help because they can see you want to help them.

What exactly then is Emotional Intelligence, or EQ?

Chapter 8

EQ: The emotional skillset that can launch or tank your students' future.

In the seminal 1995 book, ***Emotional Intelligence,*** author Daniel Goleman revealed the importance of Emotional Intelligence to success in all aspects of life. Goleman identifies five areas critical to your success: self-awareness, self-regulation, internal motivation, empathy, and social skills. Without competency in each of these five areas, your student can struggle to achieve their dreams. This can impact job satisfaction, relationships, future earning power, and even a sense of self-worth. Trying to deal with college without mastering the basics of emotional intelligence can derail your student's academic progress. This can lead to discouragement, disappointment, and dropping out of their program of study.

Here are the five core skills of Emotional Intelligence and his explanations.

Self-awareness

Goleman defines this as the ability to see and identify the emotions you are experiencing without getting wrapped up in them in the moment. He likens it to having an observer on board and in your mind. Mindfulness helps a person identify their mood, and take any actions needed to manage it for their own good at that time.

Self-regulation

This is the second aspect of dealing with your emotions. After you correctly identify your mood, you need to manage it. Science has proven what we know already; if you are angry or enraged, you can't listen or process other information. This means your student needs to have some specific coping skills for when things go wrong with the roommate(s), the big test, or the breakup with the current love interest.

Internal Motivation

More than drive, internal motivation is the ability to manage impulses, defer or delay rewards, and harness optimism as a power source to achieve and grow. At the core, it is the ability to harness your energies towards an endeavor and persevere through trials and challenges. It is the ability to get into and stay in the creative flow for the task at hand.

Empathy

According to Goleman, empathy is the ability to intuitively know how another feels. Psychiatrist Daniel Stern describes the process of attunement, often found between a parent and child, whereby a child's emotions are "met with empathy, accepted, and reciprocated". Stern and Goleman believe this process is the foundation for the important skill of empathy.

Social Skills

According to Thomas Hatch and Howard Gardner, these are the four core social skills:

- **Organizing Groups**—This is the ability (core leadership skill) of initiating and coordinating efforts of a group or a network of people.

- **Negotiating Solutions**—The skill of preventing or resolving conflicts, often found in mediators, diplomats, or arbiters.

- **Personal Connection**—A combination of empathy and connection, this is seen in good team players, excellent teachers, and dependable friends.

- **Social Analysis**—The ability to detect and/or have insights about people's motives, feelings, or concerns. This is often seen in people who seem to be everyone's personal counselor.

These great skills must be balanced by a deep awareness of one's own feelings and needs so as not create a gap between the public me and the private me.

Of course, no one has mastered all these skills. Most of us are works in progress! Still, your student's EQ is an important part of the skills needed to navigate a college or university setting. The good news is that all these skills can be learned and developed! In some cases, they may need to be re-learned, or re-coded to our minds and hearts.

Goleman stresses repeatedly that temperament, defined as the moods that typify our lives, is not our destiny. The human brain is not fully formed in childhood but continues to develop well into adulthood. There may be a default orientation towards caution or boldness, for example. Being aware of tendencies and working with your student can help hone their social skills.

Our society desperately needs people with strongly developed Emotional Intelligence. We gravitate towards and enjoy working with those who have these skills. They are prized by employers, friends, and families. So, how do you learn more about EQ, and perhaps explore it with your student? Let me share some inexpensive tests that can reveal important aspects of your student.

Time to pull back the curtain and take a peek!

Chapter 9

"Getting to know you, getting to know all about you"

—Opening line to the song,
Getting to Know You,
from the musical, *The King and I.*

When we understand how we are wired it can influence our career choices. With this information we can make better decisions about our future education and direction!

This chapter will focus on four well-known personality tests and five career aptitude tests. Please know that career counselors may favor other tests not mentioned here.

These tests can help you understand how you approach things and provide ideas for career paths based on your orientations. You can do these tests on your own or online. Be sure to do more than just one in each category, so you see the range of concepts these tests provide.

The first tool to consider is the classic Myers-Briggs personality assessment.

Myers-Briggs, developed out of research begun over a century ago, was first published in 1943. Since then it has become the grand dame of most personality tests available.

In MB, there are four personality types, consisting of four different letters, which results in sixteen separate combinations of letter types. Each type shows how a person predominantly operates in their life. These combinations create a four-letter acronym that helps us understand a bit more about one another.

Here are four categories measured by Myers-Briggs and what they indicate:

1. **How we gain our energy.** (E) Extrovert or (I) Introvert.

   The key difference between the two is the fact that Introverts gain energy by being alone and Extroverts gain it by being with others. This varies with each individual and yes, extroverts need alone time, too.

2. **How we take in information.** (S) Sensing or (N) Intuitive.

   Sensors take in information through their five senses by thinking in the here and now.

Intuitives process information by seeing patterns, possibilities, and impressions.

3. **How we make decisions.** (T) Thinking or (F) Feeling.

   A key takeaway is that Thinkers use their heads more than their hearts, while Feelers use their hearts more than their heads.

4. **Our lifestyle preference.** (J) Judging or (P) Perceiving.

   The main difference is that Judgers prefer their world structured and planned. Perceivers prefer open-ended options.

You can find a warehouse full of tests online for the Myers-Briggs system. Check to be sure there are adequate numbers of questions and be prepared to pay a small fee for the better tests. Once you know your 'type', take a few minutes to study and think about each segment. Does it correctly describe how you operate most of the time?

Whether they are an ISFJ or an ENTP, this test can show your student how they approach their world.

A second, powerful tool could be ***Strengthfinders 2.0*** by Tom Rath, which uses the Clifton method to help people identify their top strengths.

The Gallup Organization is often known only for its' Gallup polls during election cycles. However, this organization is a broad-based consulting firm advising businesses and corporations how to maximize employee strengths and skills. Here's what they found:

> "We discovered that people have several times more potential for growth when they invest energy in developing their strengths instead of correcting their deficiencies."

Strengthfinders 2.0. is the newest version of the test found in the 2001 book, **Now, Discover your Strengths.** Included in the book price is a digital key to an online test that takes between 35-45 minutes to complete. From this test, you will receive a report identifying your top five strengths. You then review your top five strengths from the thirty-four chapters in the book that describe each strength. The book, test, and results will open your mind to your best strengths and HOW you can apply them in your work and home life.

For many, reading the descriptions of their strengths and people's personal stories creates an amazing "ah-ha!" moment. For a few people, it will be an "I already knew that" type of experience. In most cases, test takers report it is the first time they feel their true self has been validated.

I remember interviewing a student one time who was smitten by the term Underwriter in a job title. I kept seeing her gifts and talents shining in a very different position. She was dismissive of my efforts to explore other available positions. Finally, I asked her why she was so interested in just one job. It turns out she thought it was a cool job title. She was paying more attention to a title and not allowing me to maximize her strengths.

Don't laugh. I am sure each of us may have done something similar. Doesn't it make sense to focus on the talents and strengths we have, and to look for educational opportunities that are more in line with our gifts?

The *Strengthfinders 2.0* process could be an exciting tool for you and your student to help identify better ways for them to learn, grow or achieve. Consider buying a book for each student and parent as it is generally affordable (well under $20). Taking your tests online individually and then sharing your results is a fun way to open up family conversations. You may even enjoy some laughs together.

Third on our list of top psychological tests, is the *Enneagram.*

Developed initially by Don Riso in 1977, the Enneagram is a circle with nine points evenly distributed around it. Each point is one of nine distinct personality types. Beginning at 1 on a clock face and going clock-wise, there are nine "numbers" around the outside of the clock face. On the inside, a series of lines connect the numbers in a specific pattern. Then, it becomes complicated.

I found the best explanation of the Enneagram at this website: https://www.enneagraminstitute.com. Their description of the Enneagram is so clear, I am sharing their website text below.

"Identifying Your Basic Personality Type"

"If taken properly, our questionnaire, the Riso-Hudson Enneagram Type Indicator (RHETI® version 2.5), will identify your basic personality type for you. This short section is included so that we can have a basic understanding of the types in our discussion without having to go to the longer descriptions in the next section.

As you think about your personality, which of the following nine roles fits you best most of the time? Or, to put it differently, if you were to describe yourself in a few words, which of the following word clusters would come closest?

The Enneagram with Riso-Hudson Type Names

These one-word descriptors can be expanded into four-word sets of traits. Keep in mind that these are merely highlights and do not represent the full spectrum of each type.

Type One is principled, purposeful, self-controlled, and perfectionistic.

Type Two is generous, demonstrative, people-pleasing, and possessive.

Type Three is adaptable, excelling, driven, and image-conscious.

Type Four is expressive, dramatic, self-absorbed, and temperamental.

Type Five is perceptive, innovative, secretive, and isolated.

Type Six is engaging, responsible, anxious, and suspicious.

Type Seven is spontaneous, versatile, acquisitive, and scattered.

Type Eight is self-confident, decisive, willful, and confrontational.

Type Nine is receptive, reassuring, complacent, and resigned.

www.enneagraminstitute.com"

After you learn your dominant number, you must take into account other factors. First, there are nine levels of psychological balance or health within each number type, as well as the influence of "wings" or neighboring numbers that may have affect your dominant trait. The result also shares in detail how your "number" or your dominant type, responds to stress.

Much like both the Myers Briggs and *Strengthfinders'*, their website states you can take this personality test for $12. It may be a good value for you if you take the time to read and review your test results.

The fourth nominee for testing consideration is the DiSC psychological profiling system. DiSC stands for Dominance, Influence (i), Steadiness, and Conscientiousness.

This system is favored by many businesses and Fortune 500 companies. DiSC is simple to understand and provides an individual profile. This system also offers specialized testing for Management, Sales and Leadership positions in a business setting.

The four core personality types are:

- **Dominance**—direct, strong-willed and forceful

- **Influence**—sociable, talkative and lively

- **Steadiness**—gentle, accommodating and soft-hearted

- **Conscientiousness**—private, analytical and logical

Think of these four types as all residing in one big circle, like a pie. Your controlling type will take up the largest share of the pie, followed by your other types in different "slice" sizes that complete the rest of your pie.

By now, you may be scratching your head. You may be thinking, "I know my kid(s) pretty well; I don't need any fancy test to tell me what I already know." Certainly, most parents are very aware of their students' wonderful ways and even more so, their endearing quirks. These tests may be more of a discovery for your student and could spark new ideas about how they can use their gifts in the real world.

Personality tests are an important starting point for each of us. The obvious, next great question we all ask is, "So, what kinds of work/careers are best for MY 'type'? There are other tests and career aptitude tests that can bring to light career options you may not know or think about. What are some well-known and highly regarded career tests available?

Todd Van Duzer, co-founder of https://www.student-tutor.com, wrote a compelling article about the top Career Aptitude tests for high school students. Excerpts from this article are shared below.

"The Myers Briggs Type Indicator, known by its' initials, MBTI, is a career assessment tool that is used by career counseling professionals. Using the same four-letter typing in the personality side of Myers Briggs, the Indicator side provides direction for you or your student to consider in looking at careers. For a fee, you can take the test online from the Center for Applications of Psychological Type or CAPT, add the career report, and have a one-hour session with a certified counselor for under $200. If you and your student are having a hard time coming up with ideas, this might be a jump start for you.

The Holland Code Career Aptitude Test, often considered the godfather of career testing, measures your interests in six areas:

- **Realistic**—mechanical, electrical, construction, working outdoors

- **Investigative**—research, experimentation, problem-solving, thinking

- **Artistic**—art, crafts, design, self-expression

- **Social**—teaching, counseling, medical care

- **Enterprising**—sales, leadership, persuasion, politics

- **Conventional**—recording, organizing, categorizing

This test promotes the idea that people like to work with others who share their skills and focus. One website, https://www.careerkey.org/, offers an online test for under $15.

"The Motivational Appraisal of Personal Potential (MAPP) Career Aptitude Test focuses on what activities gets you up and out in the mornings! This 25 year plus test is free and claims to have been done over 8 million times. You can take it at, https://www.assessment.com . It has been found to correlate well with the Strong

Interest Inventory. This test assists you in understanding what tasks you enjoy, how you work, your interactional style with others, and how you deal with your job. Total test time is between 20-30 minutes."

The Keirsey Temperament Aptitude Sorter, based on Dr. David Keirsey's model, divides people in to four temperaments:

- **Guardian**—the dutiful, focusing on achievement and traditions.

- **Idealist**—the compassionate and abstract who find deeper meaning in what they do.

- **Rational**—those who seek self-control, discipline and competence.

- **Artisan**—The optimists and fun-loving people are in this group.

These temperaments are dominant characteristics. People are influenced by these, and they can direct the core pursuits of your life. At the Keirsey website, https://www.keirsey.com, you can take a career test for just under $30.

The Princeton Review Career Quiz, a short 24 question quick take, gives you an idea of how you are focused within fifteen minutes. It divides the results as follows:

- **Green:** People-centered

- **Blue:** Ideas-centered

- **Red:** Production-centered

- **Yellow:** Procedure-centered

Designed for incoming first-year college students, some critics have viewed the Princeton test as simplistic and limitedly useful. Consider it as an addition to other career tests you plan to take.

Learning about how we work in this world, and where our gifts and talents lie, is powerful. Some people like to do tests; others would prefer to look more deeply within. If you or your student like to journal, there is a more self-guided path that can reveal your personal patterns. You may find that what makes you feel alive, special, or accomplished has deep roots within your childhood.

Let's take a trip back to a time when...

Chapter 10

The journey of a thousand miles begins with one step.

—**Lao Tzu**, Chinese philosopher and writer

For some people, the idea that they can be classified by taking a set of tests, seems—well, ridiculous. They feel they know themselves better than anyone else ever could. They are right! But when asked, we all have a hard time clearly identifying our talents, strengths, or processes we use to manage our lives.

There is another way to learn about your native and natural talents. Rather than taking a test, let's try journaling around a few key questions. This will take more time, but—with focus and effort—it should yield strong results.

Articles about self-discovery are everywhere. They are found on the web, in magazines, and throughout the social media world. To start, grab a pad of paper, a small notebook, or a journal to write down your memory stories to these four questions. TAKE your TIME! This is not a race. In fact, you may want to tackle this over a few days' time, writing each example when you remember it. Close your eyes and see your story. Capture the detail. The more you can capture, the more you will see some common threads about yourself.

Write down as many stories, anecdotes, events, or memories as you can for each question. Bring your memories to life!

Question #1—What **thrilled** you as a child? (This could be an activity, game, or an event in which you participated or attended.)

Look as far back as you can remember and write down memories that stand out because they made you feel good. What activities or memories made you giggle and laugh? What things did you do, and go back to again and again? There may be a strong memory from ages 5-6, another from 8-9, or 11-12, and so on. They all tell a story about you.

First, write down the strongest memories, ones that still stand out when you think about them. Go back to the question and remember another story. Write down how you felt after the event finished.

Question # 2—When is the last time you **lost track of time?** (Again, while you are DOING something!)

Are there activities that you do today where time passes without you noticing? What do you love to do so much you don't think about sleeping, eating, or time itself? If you can't think of anything like that today, what did that for you in the past? Each of us has experienced those moments when our world stood still, or we entered a different world altogether when we did a special activity. We felt engaged in and at one with what we were doing. This concept is known as flow. Some people call it "being in the zone".

Another clue as to your passion would be considering something you want to do so badly that you are talking about it non-stop to family and friends. In fact, they may be telling you to stop talking and start doing it! This indicates a passion in you that needs to be let out. This is another way to find talent(s) that may not have had time to emerge but are looking for an opportunity.

Question #3—What do you *yearn to do?*

What fire is burning inside you right now? It may be one thing, or it may be three things. Consider this example. Do you love to quilt and get rave reviews for your work? Great! Do you also love to get people together about a common area of interest? Super! And what if you have been journaling and writing for decades? Awesome! You might consider starting a blog or have a monthly meeting or mash-up for quilters in your area.

Taking these three talents (detailed hand work + writing + organizing) and blending them might result in something like this. You form a new group that decides to meet and donate their group time to making quilts for nursing homes in the area. Wow!

So, what personal "yearning" can you coax out of your dreams?

Question #4—What can *others tell me about my strengths, skills and talents?*

Make a list of people who you can ask that question. Talk to people who know you well and some you don't. Talk with teachers and non-parent adults you know and trust; ask them to share with you what they see in you. Tell them you are doing a self-review project and wondered if they could give you some feedback. You might say, "Can you describe my strengths, skills, and talents in ten words or less?"

Write down the words they use to see if any are similar. Try for at least ten people you know well, plus at least three people that know you in passing.

There are other excellent self-review questions besides the four above. However, I am confident that if you answer each of these questions in depth, you will start seeing words and patterns about yourself emerge. And, no opting out by saying you don't have any special talents. You do. Figuring out these things can help you focus on what you do well. When you know that, you can better direct your education, training, and find a career that draws on your best talents.

Take the time to know more about you. Shakespeare, in the play Hamlet, wrote, "... to thine own self be true." If you are to act in your own best interests, you must know what they are. And, knowing your interests and gifts is the critical step in gaining the right education for YOU.

Once you have the clues, you can flesh out the dream. There is, however, a very practical side to building that dream into your reality. Just like building any structure, you need to have core skills, and then execute those skills and processes to get you to where you want to be.

Just exactly what are those skills?

Chapter 11

Essential Skills for Your Student in High School and Beyond!

"Success in school and in life really has little to do with brains or luck and everything to do with organization, process management, and continuing to try hard every day."

—Jeannie Burlowski, author of *LAUNCH — How to get your kids through College Debt-Free and into Jobs they love afterwards*.

Jeannie Burlowski has written a fabulous roadmap for parents and students who have the wisdom to START REALLY EARLY on their college planning. As a career college and grad school academic strategist, she knows her way around this process. She advocates teaching your student skills that help them navigate school, deadlines, time management, and processes. She states this is the KEY to your student's current and future successes.

Time Management Skills

Although well covered back in Chapter 7, this cannot be overstated. Success takes planning. Managing your life takes planning on a daily, weekly, monthly, even yearly basis. "Winging it" may be exciting, but you will get burned. And, that usually happens on something important. Very little "brilliant work" is done at the last minute. Those crowded times and moments happen to everyone. But the more you have planned and done ahead, the better off you will be.

Study Skills

There are hundreds of techniques for studying. By the time you are in high school, you should know the way you need to study to do your best. Taking good notes that remind you of what you heard in class is essential. Some people are visual learners and need to doodle on their notes. It should go without saying you need to BE in class to get those notes. When you ask someone for their notes, they have written them in their own style that may be hard to interpret. Also, be smart. If you got lost during a lecture, check in with the professor/ teaching assistant for clarification. They know best what they were trying to share with you. Asking questions does NOT indicate you aren't keeping up; it shows that you care to understand.

Research Skills

As sure as the sun rises, writing college papers is a certainty. To write an A paper, you need to sharpen your research skills. What might that look like?

First, Google search is NOT the only way to get sources. In fact, in many disciplines, it is very desirable to compare original source materials.

Second—or perhaps this should be first—you have a secret and powerful weapon: the library. Yes, it is loaded with books, but most college libraries now have electronic databases specifically designed to help with student research. Make friends with the librarian. They have magical powers and love to share resources with you!

Third, be very clear on the citation format the professors want and follow it to a T. Said library may have access to citation software, too.

Finally, look at your materials, and write your paper based on your findings. Be scrupulous about using your own words and citing the works of others without fail. It alters your grade downward more than you want to know if you get this wrong.

Social/Networking Skills

College life is way better when we connect well with a core group of people we enjoy. Many lifelong friendships have been forged during this time. Yes, it takes a little bit of risk and effort to develop those relationships. For some, this comes naturally. For others a few clues and tips might help.

According to Jack Schefer, author of **The Like Switch**, just four slight body language gestures can provide "friends" signals to others. They include:

1. A genuine smile as you near a person you would like to talk to.

2. A slight raising of the eyebrow when you first see someone.

3. A small jutting out of the chin towards the person you would like to engage with.

4. Listening and reflecting back what your new friend's words helps to show that you are listening to them and acknowledge what they are saying.

That's great for when you are meeting someone, but what's next? It's good to keep in mind a handy mnemonic to help break the ice in stranger introductions. The letters F.O.R.M. which stand for Family, Occupation, Recreation and Motivation are easy to remember when you need help moving the conversation forward with someone you don't know. These are considered the socially safe areas to ask about while getting to know someone better.

Most people start with the safer Occupation question, then, moving into Recreation or Family. The Motivation question (what makes you happiest?), is often redefined into a question such as, "What do you do for fun?" Nevertheless, this is a great way to help bridge conversation gaps and start the words flowing.

Communication Skills

Communication skills are more than just writing or speaking in person. They include public presentations, guiding, and influencing others. This is a set of skills that takes practice, awareness, and self-evaluation. The first time you do any of them, you may be a bit rough around the edges. That's okay. You can improve with self-evaluation and stepping back into another opportunity.

Here are a few tips:

1. Be aware of *your own* body language. Most people you are leading or influencing want to believe in you and what you are doing. Believe this truth. Absorb it into your heart and mind. Stand or sit tall, look people in the eye, smile, and act confident. Here's the crazy good news: you can practice this in front of a mirror to get better, and you will! Science also confirms that what we "see" ourselves doing well in our mind, has the same impact as actually doing it.

Therefore, visualizing a successful presentation beforehand is a form of practice!

Tip: If you are delivering a presentation, memorize your opening statement. That gets you going, and then you can refer to your notes or speech further into the presentation.

2. Be aware of others' body language. If someone is looking away, arms folded across their ches and tapping their fingers, chances are they don't want to engage with you. If someone is looking at you, following your presentation and smiling encouragingly, then they are "getting" what you have to say. In a presentation situation, focus on the positive people. In a social setting with someone who doesn't want to be there, politely excuse yourself and move on.

3. Telling a story is almost always well received if it is presented well. If you need help with story presentation, watch a high-quality comic. They set the stage, identify the characters, set up the situation, and drop the funny on you—all in less than ninety seconds.

4. Ask questions of someone else telling a story that show you have been listening.

5. Put away distractions and devices. Taking friendship calls during an in-person conversation is seen as rude and can ruin a budding relationship.

Practice these skills in high school and you will be better able to navigate the whole new world of college and beyond.

Finally, here's my favorite, superbly written summary of what skills are needed in school, found on the Clarke University in Dubuque, IA website. You will see many topics we have already covered—no matter. It is a top-notch summary of ALL the skills and orientations required to navigate any college or university experience. Sit down and review this list with your student. Discuss each section. Let them know, like the title says,

"It's all you!"

"One of the biggest adjustments for new college students is the newfound freedom. College students have an increase in personal responsibility and a lot less external structure. There are no set study times, no required mealtimes, no one to tell them when to sleep or get them up, an increase in their academic workload, a greater need to multi-task and balance and a myriad of new social opportunities and challenges. The following are skills that will help you develop your own internal structure and be successful in college:

TIME MANAGEMENT Prepare a weekly schedule that includes time in class, studying, activities, work, meals, study and time with friends. Being a college student is like having a full-time job. Several hours of studying and preparation expected for each class.

STRESS MANAGEMENT Regular exercise, adequate rest, good nutrition, prayer and/or meditation are all suggested ways of engaging in self-care that reduces stress. Finding ways to increase coping resources will help students decrease the stressors that life will throw your way.

STUDY SKILLS Even some of the best high school students have not always developed good study skills. Knowing how to read a textbook, take notes in class, use the library and take multiple choice tests are all areas that will help you be more successful in the classroom.

MONEY MANAGEMENT It is important to have experience in independently handling money, balancing a check book, using an ATM, reading a bank statement and learning to make responsible decisions about living on a budget.

ASSERTIVENESS SKILLS Speak up for yourself in an assertive manner that is not aggressive or passively allowing others to take advantage of you. Assertiveness skills are helpful in roommate communication, study groups, teams and conflict resolution. They also involve learning and practicing healthy boundaries.

WELL-DEVELOPED SELF CARE SKILLS Develop bedtimes based on physical need and health. Adequate sleep and a healthy diet can improve mood, athletic and classroom performance and coping strategies for stress. Exercise, relaxation and good hygiene are also important aspects of self-care.

KEEPING SAFE AND AVOIDING RISKY BEHAVIORS Staying safe means learning to advocate for your wellbeing. It means making smart and low-risk choices and planning for the "what ifs" in life.

SEEKING ASSISTANCE WHEN NEEDED A big part of advocating for yourself is knowing when to ask for help. The college years are a time for learning new information, new life skills and a new way of relating with our world. Seeking help when you need it is a sign of strength and integrity, not an admission of failure.

RESPECTING THE RULES AND POLICIES Every community has rules and policies and our college campus is no different. Our rules and policies apply to safety and fostering a positive community where all students are respectful of themselves, others and the environment.

DISPLAYING HONESTY, INTEGRITY AND PERSEVERANCE Learning to incorporate personal values and ethics into every aspect of life is a significant part of personal growth during the college experience. Part of the path of integrity is learning how to hang in there and stay committed to goals."

There's a BIG reason for taking these life management skills to heart. They can make the difference between earning that degree or walking out with a mountain of debt and no paper. When you learn about the true four-year and six-year graduation rates at our colleges and universities, all this will make sense.

Question; Are your odds better gambling the college fund money in Vegas or investing in your student in college? You may be surprised at the answer!

Chapter 12

Your chances of graduating with any degree may be worse than Vegas odds, baby!

If graduation rates were the only measure of student success at our colleges or universities, most would be given a failing grade. This is a well-hidden tidbit about our institutions of higher learning. It simply isn't discussed. You and your student deserve to know the reality you are facing on this important issue. It is critical if you are borrowing money to send them to school.

To be fair; it is NOT the educational institution's responsibility to ensure the graduation of all their enrolled students. At least, not entirely. The problem has many facets, and the issue of graduation is affected by many variables. It would be fair to say that there is enough blame to go around.

BEFORE I share numbers with you, you need to understand the Federal definition of graduation rates. This number only includes first-time, full-time students who are in a group (those entering in the same year) who actually graduate within a 150% of the expected time to graduate. That would be six years on the four-year plan or three years on the two-year plan. Whoa. So, these graduation rates are based on six year and three years, you ask? Yes. Keep reading.

Also, this graduation rate does not include part-time students, non-traditional (online), transfer students, or drop-outs. It can be argued that this eliminates a vast group of real people doing college in stages and phases. This suggests the actual graduation rates for ALL students at an institution may be even lower or longer.

It is not hard to see this narrowly focused number skews graduation rates higher for two groups of schools. First, the more traditional (private sector) in which most students are full time, and second, the more selective (schools that accept less than 25% of their applicants) programs.

According to the Data Dashboard at the https://www.completecollege.org website, the statistics are grim indeed. Getting a four-year degree, IN four years, ranges from a low of 10% to a high of 42% of those initially enrolled. The six-year completion numbers range from 33% to 71%. Their charts are also broken down by gender and ethnicity.

The national average graduation rate at six years remains around 61%. Amazing. Once again, let's be clear; the highest number who graduate in four years is ONLY four out of ten students. The best number two years later is just at seven out of ten. That means that three out of every ten students are not graduating, period.

To combat this selective data, a different study was done. The National Student Clearinghouse (NSC) undertook a rigorous six-year college completion study that tracked individual students entering college in the fall of 2011, all the way through to 2018. In Forbes magazine, Preston Cooper wrote an article detailing the results of this study. In it he says, "No one should consider a 57% aggregate college completion rate ideal." That's right. When they followed ALL the entering students—over 200,000—only 57% earned any degree in seven years. Seven years. Are you kidding me?

How do the different types of colleges rank? Mr. Cooper singles out four-year, for-profit colleges as among the worst with a regular completion rate of just under 35%. The public community colleges have a national completion rate of just 38%, even after transfers away to four-year schools are taken into account.

The hidden story of all of this can be seen in the next, sad set of numbers. There are 31.1 million Americans who have some college credit and no degree. A large portion of those former students also have college loans that must be repaid. No degree and lots of debt is a financial millstone hung around their necks.

There is ample evidence as to why students get in this mess. The two leading causes for those thirty-one million Americans with some credits and no degree has not changed in decades. They are shaky finances and academic unpreparedness. We have shown the need for academic readiness, work ethic, and skills training in previous chapters. This entire book is dedicated to help you build a solid plan for doing college or technical training as close to debt-free as possible.

If you want to see how much graduations can vary right in your neighborhood, check out all the schools in the area around where you live. If you want to compare colleges' 4 and 6-year graduation rates, including a breakdown of student populations by ethnicity, income, and gender, use the http://www.collegeresults.org website. This website uses the Federal government's numbers, so take that into account. Even so, it will give you a better idea of which schools will provide your best graduation chances within your budget.

These realities should help everyone become very clear about the odds for your student. Maybe it is time to take an open-minded look at options that are not well-known?

What if there IS A WAY TO:

- Earn college credits for up to two years at nearly 80% of all universities and colleges?

- Pay between 10-25% of college tuition in your area and to earn the exact same credits?

- Be able to work and save money for your next phase of education while you are doing this?

Yes, there is. It is one of the best-kept secrets in education out there. Time to pull back the curtain and let the light in on the magic.

SECTION THREE

Cost Savvy Options for Families and Their Students

Chapter 13

I am like most of you. No one told me about this, either.

The big push when our daughter was in high school was AP courses. She did them. She worked so hard to get good grades. She took the national exams, earning a few course credits towards her college general studies classes. But, her scores from her sophomore year AP exams in high school were NOT high enough to get any college credits. And the worst part was not finding that out until she was going to attend her university, two years later.

Had we known this next secret, she could have taken a different exam at a low cost, and likely would have scored well enough for credits anywhere. What is it? CLEP! CLEP stands for College Level Exam Placement. Let's walk through this option.

These are college credits you can earn while you are in high school, after high school, during a gap year, or even during college. The cost of the test and study materials is under $200 for each course. Over 2,900 of the 3,500+ colleges and universities in the United States accept them. Each school sets their own list of accepted courses AND their required passing grade in each course.

In the interest of full disclosure, let's be clear. Many flagship universities and some selective private schools do NOT participate in this program. We must respect their right to make that decision. Nevertheless, almost six out of seven schools DO accept these credits. Because a huge portion of the two million freshmen attend schools that do accept these courses, CLEP is a major game changer.

CLEP is a part of and administered by the well-respected College Board. This is a national subject matter test, and the highest score you can achieve is an eighty. Most schools accept a grade ranging between fifty and fifty-five.

Here's the critical point: **you must KNOW which school you will attend for your final two years of college.** Each school establishes which CLEP courses they accept, and what passing grade is required. To make this work, you will need to know you will be admitted to the school around which you build your personal CLEP program.

Many colleges and Universities have their CLEP list online. This is often found in an obscure part of the academic section of their website. If you can't find it, call the school for a list of CLEP credits courses they accept. THEN, you build your CLEP program around your school's available CLEP courses and their general studies requirements. DO NOT go signing up for courses through CLEP without first seeing which ones will be accepted at YOUR school of choice.

The national exam fee for a three-credit course currently costs under $120. This is administered in a professional testing center, on campus at a local community college, university, or in a nearby city. The College Board provides study materials at a cost of $60 per topic.

The average exam typically takes 90-120 minutes, and you'll know your score instantly. Remember all that matters is earning the passing grade required by the school you will be attending.

What kind of CLEP program could your student develop in a twelve-month period of time? They could identify the required general courses in their school of choice and check the classes against accepted CLEP credits. They would then start studying and taking exams for those classes.

Let's review what a traditional college student takes. The average student takes four courses a semester, or eight in an academic year. If you bought the study guides, took sixteen CLEP exams over a two-year period and passed them all, your cost would be under $3,200. Can you believe that? Under $200 per three-credit course. Depending on where you live, that might be just 10% to 25% of local college or university tuition.

Yes, you heard that right. You can take care of most of your first two years of general courses for between a tenth or a quarter of the tuition costs of your local public university.

And no one talks about it. Why? Because it is not in their best interest. Remember in Chapter 1, I said they required BICs? Yes, that is Bottoms in Chairs. If you are not in their chair, you are not paying them money to be there.

To make this work you must plan carefully. Here are the steps you need to take to make this an actionable process.

- You must identify the college or university you *will* attend, and you need to know your student's major. Getting accepted is important. You can always defer entering the school until later. Review the major study requirements in the chosen school's catalog, against the list of accepted CLEP courses. Draw up a plan. Connect with an academic counselor at the school to review your plan and confirm your choices will receive credits at their institution.

- Your student must plan to study up on the selected subject, set an exam date and take and pass the exam at the level required by their institution of choice. If you do not pass your first time, CLEP has a rule that you cannot re-take a subject test for six months. It would be smart to start with a couple of strong subjects from high school to gauge the amount of study needed to pass.

- Assuming you were successful, tweak the plan (more or less studying needed) and repeat. If you can take one exam every six weeks for a year, you could earn eight classes' worth of credits each year.

This only works if your student has the academic readiness and discipline to tackle this program. The goal of earning a Bachelors' degree for the least possible cost to you and to them must remain top of mind for all involved.

There is an old adage that you need to study two hours for every one hour of class instruction in college. If you were in class three hours a week in college, you received about forty-two hours of instruction time. Your total learning time on a subject might be 120-130 hours. That is around twenty hours a week on a course of study, if you plan to take an exam every six weeks.

In a 52-week year, you could complete eight courses in one year, and take four weeks off!

To get a more detailed picture of CLEP, go to https://clep.collegeboard.org.

Not only is this a fantastic deal, there is an even MORE fantastic deal available. Check out this website, https://modernstates.org/freshman-year-free/. Modern States, in collaboration with renowned college professors, has funded top-quality online lecture courses on ALL the available CLEP subjects. All you do is sign up with Modern States, do the free course lectures, apply and receive a free testing voucher, and take your exam locally. It doesn't get much better than that! (Just don't forget to study!)

In a nutshell, they are offering free online CLEP courses and waiving testing fees in the Freshman Year Free program. If you are serious about trying this path, this is the zero to low cost way to try it!

Whoa. Wait a moment. You may have a hard time seeing your student doing college this way. Somehow, this is not what you envisioned.

Yes, I know. This is not the college you remember, or even wish was still available. I really understand that, because a part of me feels exactly the same. The world has changed a lot since some of us were in school. The biggest change is unfortunately an insane price tag we can't afford that anymore.

Yes, I know. Something will be missing, doing it this way. What about gaining new friends? Or, having in-person spirited academic discussions, and those fun antics of campus life? Is that lost with this approach? To a large degree, it is—at least for the first two years. However, if you are working towards going to traditional university for your final two years, and you have been working and saving to do so, hurray! Going into life-limiting debt to experience four years of campus life is hard to justify anymore.

Now more than ever, we must help our students by saying, "Enough"! We must be open to alternatives for financially managing the cost of college today.

As they say on the game shows, "But WAIT! There's more!" Indeed, there are a variety of other ways to do college for free, or very inexpensively! Let's take a fresh look at some well-known and then NOT so well-known alternatives.

Chapter 14

Two roads diverged in a wood and I-I took the one less traveled by, and that has made all the difference.

—Robert Frost

Indeed, it can make ALL the difference. CLEP is the most amazing option that no one knows about or uses. Check. Now, let's review many other options that might work with your student.

Dual-enrollment option

In many high school districts, students can interview at the end of their sophomore year to enter a Dual Enrollment Program. Dual Enrollment generally refers to being enrolled in high school and in college at the same time. This program is paid for by the school district and provides general studies college credits that are transferable to a college or university upon high school graduation. This dual enrollment option is often controlled by a tough application and interview processes. Not all students who apply are selected. Taking and passing college level courses in your Junior and Senior years in high school takes a lot of work and focus. Not every student is ready and willing to commit to that.

While this is a great program and can save a student and their family a lot of money, there are some things to keep in mind about this special program.

- Students are often selected from an applicant pool across a school district. Academic achievement in the first two years of high school is a large part of the selection criteria. Because there are limited slots, competition can be fierce.

- Extra-curricular activities such as band, football, basketball, or drama still take place at the student's old high school. Dual enrollment courses are often taught at a college or university campus that may not be next door to your student's high school. Some school systems will have a bus take your student back to their original high school, where a "late" bus then picks them up and transports them home after the extra-curricular activity. This could put your student getting home an hour or more later than if they attended their regular high school. For students with these interests, be sure to get a clear picture of how this works for you.

- Specialty courses in Art, Music, and Drama are often NOT a part of the dual enrollment program. If your student is committed in those directions, be sure to ask about access to those programs while attending the Dual Enrollment courses where you live.

- If your student plans to attend colleges and universities in your state, those credits will likely transfer in. That is a great benefit. However, now your student has only two years, not four to meet their requirements for their major area of study,

Your student should make an appointment with an academic advisor when they arrive on campus as a Junior. Their major area of study requirements could include courses that are only taught once every two years. If you are not careful, your student might "miss" a required course, causing them to need to stay longer.

This happened to a student friend of ours. She "missed" a required course in the fall semester of her junior year. She had to take it in her fifth year in order to make a pushed-back December graduation.

Have your student re-check with the counselor at the end of each quarter or semester to confirm their on-time progress. This is to make sure no new required courses have popped up that have not been accounted for in their plan.

Community College Option

This educational path continues to be under-appreciated, misunderstood, and ignored. We can no longer afford that kind of thinking. Community college is a terrific option for many. It is a lower cost alternative to universities, a gateway to technical and trade careers, and usually a good place to polish your academic skills.

Let's talk technical skills education options. In the world of machinists, welders, and jobs such as aircraft maintenance, jobs are going begging. Highly skilled craftsmen and women are retiring in record numbers right now. Entire industries and companies are scrambling for their replacements. If you have a student with a gift for mechanical, construction, or diesel machinery work, the world can be a great place for them in high demand technical occupations.

Here's what's happening. Local companies are partnering with the local community college systems. They set up a program to train selected students on the skills those employers need. Selected (and yes, you must be interviewed and selected) students ARE PAID to attend classes and training. Tuition costs are paid by the consortium of businesses. While the length of study and training vary widely by area and interest, the students come out:

*Debt-Free

*Certified

*With multiple job offers from many potential employers!

Check in to your local community college to see if your student might shine in such a program.

In almost all cases, community colleges cost roughly a third to half the cost of a public university system school. Your student can attend school full-time, and likely find work that can flex around their classes.

Military Education Options

Yes, there are plenty of programs and choices! Higher education options are available to both active-duty members of the military and veterans. Let's take a "411" quick facts tour that applies to every branch of service, including Coast Guard.

As a general guideline, you cannot begin taking courses until after ninety days of active service. Each service branch will have its' own conditional requirements and caps on credit hours (or dollars) allowed per year.

Here's what they offer:

Tuition Assistance

In general, Tuition Assistance pays up to 100 percent of the cost of tuition or expenses up to a maximum of $250 per credit hour. A total of $4,500 per year is available. In the next section, you can see some credit hour charges for various online schools. A decent number of schools don't charge that much for online credit hours. Still, if your per-credit cost was $200, you could earn twenty-two credits a year. That might be between six or seven courses per year. It may take a little longer to complete your degree (if you need around 130 credit hours to graduate), but it can be completely paid for by the military. Please note selected Reserve and National Guard units offer Tuition Assistance, but the benefits vary from this program.

The Post-9/11 GI Bill

In effect since 08/01/2009, this is the most comprehensive GI bill rewrite since the original law in 1944. This is available to veterans who have served since 09/10/2001, with at least ninety days continuous service and who received an honorable discharge. Reserve and Guard members with more than ninety days active service since 9/11 have the same full benefit as identified below.

This Post-9/11 GI bill pays all public school in-state tuition and fees, not to exceed the highest public college and university fees and tuition in each state. In other words, they will pay up to the most expensive in-state fees and tuition charged in *your* state.

A Living Costs Stipend equal to the basic housing allowance in that zip code for an E-5 with dependents is provided to the veteran, also. And, an allowance for books and supplies ($1,000 per year) is also granted.

Colleges and universities that participate in the Yellow Ribbon Program offer additional funding towards educational costs that are above the benefits outlined in the Post 9/11 GI Bill. This can stretch your dollars. However, you might consider comparing this program with other military education benefit programs to get the right fit.

Sharing Benefits with Family

When a service member commits to additional military service time, a service member can transfer all or part of her/his earned benefits to their spouse and children. This "pass around" benefit is a first for the GI bill and expands family education opportunities. Details vary, so you need to visit the Veterans Affairs site, or talk with a recruiter of the military branch that interests you.

College Fund Program

These programs are first offered to service members when they join the Military. Often known as the GI Bill "kicker", they provide additional money that can be added to individual GI Bill benefits. Since incentives and amounts vary by branch of service, again, you need to get the details from the Veterans Affairs site or a recruiter.

Loan Repayment Program (for those entering the military with loan debt.)

Both the Army and Navy offer programs of college loan repayment to help enlisted personnel with loans taken out prior to entering military service. Once again, they vary by service branch; all are designed to help recent college graduates manage their educational debt. Loans generally need to be current. The maximum debt repayment is $65,000, and the loans need to have been Department of Education guaranteed student loans. It sounds like a broken record, but see a recruiter for details.

As you can see, the military system has some well-designed options for helping your student either pay back Federal loans (versus private loans) or getting their degree while working and serving in the military. Incentives, signing bonuses, and other benefits vary by the needs of the military at the time your student may enlist. If this is a viable option for you and your family, be sure to get in touch with a recruiter and learn all you can. It might be a great fit.

Online Degree Options

Ever since the Internet took off twenty years ago, educational delivery of information has been changed forever. Even the words podcast, webinars, online classes, weren't in the dictionary back then. But they are today. And they will be in the future.

There are many great websites that can get you started on the journey of exploring an online degree. Check out:

- https://www.bestcolleges.com

- https://www.affordablecollegesonline.org

But, before you take that step, be sure you are asking all the right questions. Skipping this part of the process could waste your money and your time. Without verification, you might end up with a worthless degree.

Here are the important issues to cover:

Accreditation

This REALLY matters. Accreditation means the school your student attends has had their curriculum and instructors reviewed by an outside group of educators. There are lots of schools who say they are accredited—or worse, provide false accreditation credentials. How are you supposed to know? While the U.S. Department of Education is NOT charged with accreditation of colleges and universities, they DO provide a database that identifies who are the accreditation commissions in your area. Check out the name of the regional commission or state commission at your local university. Then, go to the Department of

Education's website and type in the school. The web address for this is: https://ope.ed.gov/dapip/ #/home. Write down the name of the accrediting commission for a state school, and then compare that with the school of your choice.

Another and critical factor for being sure your choices are accredited is the money. No accreditation, no federal student aid is available. Beware: If you are only offered private loans, the school you have chosen may not be accredited by the regional accreditation commission. That could be trouble down the road.

Transferability of Credits (and, acceptance of any CLEP courses you have done!)

When you have narrowed your search to your top three online programs, then you can ask these questions of any online program.

- Will your program accept Advanced Placement Credits and at what scoring levels?

- Will your school accept CLEP credits, and at what passing grades?

- Will your online school accept course credits from XYZ school you attended before?

Basically, you want to know how far into the degree journey you can start, to save yourself even more money.

Academic Support and/or Guidance

Online studies can be great, but if you find yourself stuck, how do you get needed help? Be sure you find out about how your online school handles this area. You won't be the first student who needs some help. In most cases, you can reach out to your professor or instructor. If your need includes more intense academic tutoring, be sure your program has that available and you understand how to use it.

Course Delivery Systems and the Technology YOU need.

You need an up-to-date computer (a laptop less than three years old is ideal for studying in various places) and solid access to the internet to attend school this way. This may be one of your first college investments, so choose wisely for your program needs.

Learn about how the course is delivered to you, the student. For example, some courses are Synchronistic, meaning they require you to attend online at a certain time of day. Others are delivered Asynchronistically, which means that you attend recorded lectures and take online exams when it is convenient for you. Some courses blend the two delivery systems. Be sure you are VERY clear that the program you are signing up for is a good fit for you and your schedule. Because you may need to be working and going to school online, this is a critical issue to understand and be able to manage.

Helping you know your costs for online studies is a top feature of https://www.bestcolleges.com. They have a whole section focused on affordability and they show the cost either by credit hour or by the year. As you start narrowing down your online degree options, create a spreadsheet that compares the costs per credit hour. Most semester-based colleges and universities require between 120 and 130 credit hours to graduate. Schools that use a quarter system require around 180 credits. Don't be put off by that. It is the same work, but credit hours are counted differently.

Online studying is gaining ground in acceptance and popularity. Well-respected Universities now offer robust online programs. You must look carefully at the cost, the delivery method of educational content, and your student's ability to do college this way.

The traditional path to and through college has many neighboring paths today. It is hard to commit to any path without first knowing how much money you have available when you start. Money, or the lack of money, always impacts ALL our decisions.

Would some Action Guides based on how much money you have in hand help?

I thought so. Read on!

Chapter 15

"If you don't know where you are going, any road can take you there."

—Cheshire Cat, *Alice's Adventures in Wonderland*

It is not fair to tell you all the challenges, show you some options, and just say good luck. I won't leave you hanging out there to dry.

Instead, I want to remind you once again of the core values and beliefs that are the guiding principles behind this book. Then, the final three chapters are Action Guides based on the range of money you have available to your student. Chapter 16 is for students with $0-10,000 available. Chapter 17 is for students with $10,001-20,000 available. Chapter 18 is for $20,001-30,000 available.

When you are on a serious budget, every dollar counts. Every skill matters. Your student must be fully involved in the plan to get them through as debt-free as possible; I suggest you work through the plan together. This makes for much stronger buy in and ownership.

Let's review the process together:

Get them through the RIGHT school

Taking time to select the right school is critical to your cost managing process. When you know *why* your student is in school, *what* they want to study and become, and *where* they will thrive, you have found the right school. Occasionally, changing colleges and universities is necessary. Rarely is it done without great expense and disruption. Sadly, it often results in loss of earned college credits. Statistically, it also lowers their chances of EVER graduating with a degree. Give this part your full attention and direction to do all you can to avoid needing a college transfer option.

At the BEST possible price

No or very low debt is a critical goal to your student's future. The incredible freedom of no college debt creates the greatest options for them when they graduate. It reduces stress on their future plans. It helps them to move forward into relationships, establishing homes, and going on with life. Low or reduced debt allows them the best chance at living their best life.

In the LEAST amount of time

Time is money in this arena. So, plan your time to save your money. Review your plan to include any prior CLEP credits, AP credits, dual-enrollment credits. Don't forget to compare their plan with the course catalog from your school of choice. These catalogs are usually very accurate, but you should trust AND verify with the school. After all, if something is overlooked, your wallet will have to be opened again.

That results in a DEGREE or CERTIFICATION they can use.

Your goal is to support your student becoming a graduate with a degree OR the appropriate certification. I can think of nothing worse than almost making it through. Even if you have spent carefully and done the work, your future is limited until you cross the finish line! Cross the finish line!

This is why I have prepared these Action Guides for you. Don't be surprised that they offer similar advice. That is because the impact of $30,000 saved for college may not be much better than $10,000 in today's economy. Extra money buys just a little more flexibility and options.

Now, which Action Guide is the right one for you and yours?

Chapter 16

ACTION GUIDE—For students with $0 to $10,000 to invest towards school.

Welcome to a large group of people. Yes, that's right. In spite of what you may hear, *many* people have not been able to put away a lot of money for college for their students. Life can get in the way. Just know you have more company than you may realize.

These Action Guides are very honest and very realistic. They may not be the dream your student envisioned. If you have not discussed money with your student, this difficult conversation must happen now. I am confident if you tell them you both will work on a plan to help them get this done, that will go a long way towards taking some of the sting out of this tough conversation.

A. Work to earn money. It is a reality that this budget won't get you too far in to your college program. However, take heart. Just two years of thirty hours a week work at $15/hour average pay, will result in $22,500 gross income per year. You could, with low living costs, put away some $30k towards college after two years of working thirty hours a week. This still gives you plenty of room for study, and even some fun times.

B. Keep living costs super low. Consider living at home while working, and paying nominal rent, utilities and food costs. If you can't stay at home, share a room in a modest apartment with a friend or friends. Give yourself a real low allowance each week. Hide your college money from yourself by making it hard to get to easily. Behave like a poor college student, because you are one.

C. Invest in a quality computer, internet access, and a printer. You will need all three to do your college work, study for CLEP exams, and write papers. There are very good laptops out there for under $800. Printers are reasonable, too.

D. Try your first CLEP study and exam in a subject at which you did well in school. Be sure you get the coaching materials, study them, and take the exam. Don't forget to sign up for the free testing voucher from the Modern States website. If you don't pass, see if you can figure out what went wrong. Target taking and passing a CLEP test every six weeks.

E. Consider investing in tutoring for college level study skills. Knowing how to study saves you time and money. Many smart students who did well in high school lack real study skills. Some go off to college where they do poorly because they have never learned the right way to study. Check out tutoring centers for courses or a training process on this issue. If you weren't a strong student in high school, this is important to address before you get bogged down.

F. If you are in a technical or trade program, follow the path set out before you. They have the process down to a science. Trust the process. If you are accepted to a specialized training program where you get paid to attend class and train, you are in a great spot! Follow the program and stay on track!

G. Keep your next step goals in front of you. Plan your work and work your plan. I won't sugar coat it; this takes discipline on your part. Be sure you take a little time and a wee bit of money to celebrate your milestone successes. If we don't celebrate ourselves, who will?

H. Check out your employer's benefits package to see if tuition reimbursement is on the plan. Newsflash! Walmart and McDonalds are offering college tuition assistance. Walmart offers Live Better U, a program for full, part-time and manager associates for a total cost of $1 a day, or $365 per year. Their online course offerings come from six universities and include fourteen programs. They also provide ACT/SAT prep, pay for books, tuition, and more.

McDonald's offers between $2,500 and $3,000 per year for tuition reimbursement to full-time and part-time associates and managers. Review the options your employer may have, (including how you stay "qualified" to receive this benefit) and take advantage of them! At this point, every dime someone else will pay you or reimburse you, lets you keep more money for you.

At the end of two years, you could end up with $30,000 plus in the bank, 40-60 CLEP credits, and the ability to pay for a good part of your next two years in college. It will take careful planning, low living costs, and a lot of personal discipline. Yes, you may need to work for living expenses while going to college. Many do. But, if you stay the course, you could graduate with little to no debt.

Make no mistake. Employers LOVE to hire people with this kind of story. It shows goal setting, hard work, discipline, and stick-to-it-ness. Being able to work and get that degree is a BIG accomplishment. That self-discipline makes you a top employment prospect down the road!

Chapter 17

ACTION GUIDE—For students with $10,001-20,000 to invest towards school.

So, congratulations are in order. This money range gives you a few more options to work through. For example, you might choose to go full-time to a Community College and work fewer hours part time.

A. Yes, you still need to work! Even if you get into an "earn and learn" trade skills program that is tuition and debt free to you, you need to bank money. If you think you don't need to work, watch that $20,000 disappear quickly. Pay as you go is the best path whenever that option is available.

B. Keep living costs low. This is not a time to splurge on a fancy apartment or a brand-new car. (If your car dies, get a quality used one!) Even with your cushion, think and operate like a starving college student. Again, if you can stay home, it will let you bank a lot of money.

C. Invest in a quality laptop, printer and internet service. There are terrific computers out there without the "name brand" attached. Check out the online reviews. Plan for your system to last for at least four years, so choose and invest wisely.

D. Work the CLEP system. Again, unless you are in a trade skills program, aim your CLEP studies towards the school you will be attending (checking this out in advance with their Admissions Department). You will have to develop your own study and test and pass system. Start on a subject you did well in and branch out.

E. Consider hiring a tutor for study OR subject skills. If you need subject matter help, the same tutoring centers can usually help with that also. Yes, it costs money. Fine. Paying for tutoring on a subject or on study skills still costs way less than flunking a college course at full price.

F. Stay committed to any skills or trades training program. The road can seem so long in the middle of any course of study. It is exciting at the beginning and the end, but what a grind it is in the middle. To overcome this, shorten your focus on what needs to be done tomorrow, next week, next month.

G. Milestones need to be celebrated! Celebrate your first CLEP course passed! Then, celebrate more credits! Celebrate saving an additional $10,000 or $15,000. In other words, celebrate reaching markers and milestones on this journey.

H. Employer tuition benefits should be maximized. What do you need to do to get to this free money? Do it! Tell your story of working your way through school to be debt-free. It might win you a scholarship! Any time you can apply for money, take the chance. Speak from your heart on any essay required. Tell the story of your journey to earn your degree while working to stay out of debt. Be aware that testing for CLEP credits may NOT qualify for tuition reimbursement with your employer. Find out. Compare their program and costs with *your* plan, to see what makes sense to you and your savings program. Don't spend more on their program just to get some reimbursement.

At the end of working for two years, you may have $30-35,000 banked. Likely, you will still need to work in your last two years of school. But the extra money may let you cut back on hours needed while in school. Again, keep in mind the goal of getting out with a degree/certification DEBT-FREE!

Chapter 18

ACTION GUIDE—For students with $20,001-30,000 to invest towards school

It's pretty simple and pretty obvious. The more money in the bank, the more education options you may see for yourself. True. Just remember that you are not just working for today's costs, but for your final two years in college.

A. Yes, you still need to work! I know. You might be thinking you are sitting pretty and have plenty of money. When you break it down you have between $5,000 and $7,500 per year. That might pay for community college tuition. There's living expenses, books, commuting costs, and other expenses. You want to be sure you are covering ALL your costs through work.

B. Keep living costs low. If possible, live at home the first two years. Once again, think frugal. Even with your cushion, think and operate like a starving college student. Every time you can reduce your expenses, it is money in the bank to help keep you loan free.

C. Invest in a quality laptop, printer, and internet service. No matter what program you choose, you need quality tools to get the work done. Shop for steal deals by considering less well-known brands that rate well for durability.

D. Work the CLEP system. If you can earn college credits for less than 20% of the university charges, why wouldn't you? Aim your CLEP studies towards the school you will be attending. You will have to develop your own study, test, and pass system. Seriously. THIS is THE secret sauce for saving you buckets of money. This is money you need down the road for more school and a good life.

E. Consider tutoring for study OR subject skills. It is much less expensive to get skills or subject matter training. Yes, it costs money. Fine. But, if it helps you pass a CLEP exam, you have saved thousands in college or university tuition and fees. That's your money truth every time you pass the CLEP subject exam.

F. Stay committed to any skills or trades training program. The road can seem so long in the middle of any course of study. It is exciting at the beginning and the end, but what a grind in the middle. This elephant is best eaten one bite at the time. Focus on today, tomorrow, this week, next week, and this month's goals.

G. Milestones need to be identified and celebrated! College is a long journey. Celebrate your first CLEP course passed! Then, celebrate earning twenty credits! Celebrate saving every $10,000 or $15,000 in traditional education costs. In other words, celebrate reaching markers and milestones on this journey.

H. Employer tuition benefits should be maximized. Whatever you need to do to receive this free money, do it! Tell your story of working your way through school to be debt-free. It might win you a scholarship! Any time you can apply for money, take the chance. Speak from your heart. Sometimes your path, doing it the CLEP way, may NOT qualify for tuition reimbursement. Don't fall for the temptation to stop your personal CLEP program just to use their money. Compare their program and costs with *your* plan, to see what makes sense to you. Do your math.

In the end, your success in this process is developing your plan AND working your plan. Write it down. Share your plan. Have accountability partners who will keep you focused. Drill down in your plan so you know what you need to EVERY week. Execute every day. Then take some time to enjoy, recharge, and do it again.

Epilogue

It is my heart's hope that you are empowered by learning the truth and the options available to you and your student. My goal is to show you a different, less costly path towards the educational training, degrees, or certifications that are right for your student. My fervent hope is that you can launch your student forward into their gifts and calling in our world. When the right people using their best gifts are educated well, our world changes for the better.

I am calling on each of you to be real for yourself and your student. If you or your student are not ready to do this right now, that is fine. Go out and work for a while and see what you want to do. That is an honorable path. Have the strength to call your truths.

If your reality is, "I am not financially ready to do this", that is okay. You can change that in a couple of years working and saving. Or, if you're thinking, "I am not ready to sit in classes right now"–no problem. Work so you can make that choice later.

Due to increases in longevity, our students might be working for 45-50 years. What does it matter if you take a couple of years to earn CLEP credits and work, so you come out at or near debt-free? It means you are a brilliant consumer. You are shopping for the most cost-effective education that is right for you.

Keep working to change the way you get the education you need for your dreams.

Please know that I'll be right here, cheering you on. In fact, I'd love to hear your success stories and all about your hard-won journeys! Hit me up on Facebook, Twitter or Instagram with your great stories. Let's show everyone your commitment to:

- Get them through the RIGHT school;

- At the BEST possible price;

- In the LEAST amount of time;

- That results in a DEGREE or CERTIFICATION they can use!

Grace and Peace,

Bonnie Burkett

Acknowledgements

If it takes a village to raise a child, it most certainly takes one to raise an author, My only fear about this section is that I will leave someone out who has had a part in my journey. If you are that person, I beg your forgiveness up front.

Decades ago, Dr. Ben Farley wrote on a paper that I had a "book or two in me." While I doubt this is what he meant, the memory has simmered deep in the back of my mind for decades. The original starter materials came together in a training course I designed. The overwhelming response in my classes suggested a great hunger for this kind of information.

I started "tossing the idea out" among friends and family. The more I talked about it, the more excited I got, Finally, that tipping point came when my dearest friend looked at me and said, "Enough, already! Why don't you write the book?"

Thank you, Nancy Coen Hendricks for pushing me over the edge. Melissa Thompson, you blazed the path ahead for me, and as I watched publish your best seller, The

Me Disease, I believed for the first time, I might be able to do this too.

Jean Yerian, a lifetime friend and great cheerleader, was a fount of knowledge I tapped for information on both personality and career testing options. I hope I did you proud.

My stellar team at work who have done just fine without me for those countless times I came home to "work on it a little more." You guys are the best.

I joined the Self Publishing School Community, and have been blessed with stellar, positive connections there. My writing coach, Lise Cartwright, editor Lizette Balsdon, and formatter Debbie Lum are top notch professionals with a passion to take me to the finish line.

So grateful for our loving and caring daughter who granted permission for parts of her story to surface in a few pages. She also gave input to her Dad on the cover design, and in general reassured me I was doing fine,

And, finally, a salute to my wonderful husband, David. He eagerly stepped up to get the cover done, design & format the graph, etc. But more than that—he cooked, he did laundry, and he kept cheering me on through this process. He is a true and loving partner in our adventure called life together. I could not do this without him.

Made in the USA
Coppell, TX
02 October 2022